PRAISE FOR
BOOKWORM BABI

"The world needs more readers — and thinkers! *Bookworm Babies* is a treasure trove of insight and strategies on how to go beyond simply reading. Activating the full potential of a book requires a bit of practice — as well as inspiration. Kimberly Zimmer Aulenback and Dawn Ohanian Tringas have created a very special book that gives parents and educators a big dose of both practical ideas and inspiration. Bravo!"

— Peter Reynolds
Award-Winning Author and Illustrator

"*Bookworm Babies* is a must-read for new parents! It contains exactly the information caregivers need to start their little ones on a lifetime journey filled with a love for literacy and learning. It speaks in a simple, caring and very personal way to the reader. The book shares the important elements of not only why it is so vital to read with children starting in infancy, but how to read with children. The combination of the why and the how creates a book that not only gives the reader confidence to begin the ritual of reading with their child but the enthusiasm and inspiration to start right away!"

— Beth Donegan Driscoll, M.S., CCLS
Director of Child Life Services, Boston Children's Hospital

"I absolutely loved reading this book. It is thoughtful, insightful, and filled with wonderful ideas for new parents to give their child the best start of all, with books! A love of reading starts when a caring adult opens the world between the pages of a book. Every parent should have this one!"

— Vicki C. Milstein, M.S.Ed.
Principal of Early Education, The Public Schools of Brookline, MA
Author of *Integrating Math into the Early Childhood Classroom*

"*Bookworm Babies* offers tools to be fully engaged with children as we share experiences, bond, and create a love for learning and reading. The *Bookworm Babies* Method is a great way to work on critical thinking and story schemas as they relate to early reading comprehension."

— Dr. Laurie Cestnick, Ph.D.
Neuroscientist of Reading and Dyslexia at Harvard University and MIT
Pediatric Psychologist

"Most parents will read to their children without thinking about how they are doing so. *Bookworm Babies* provides excellent guidance to these parents to not only make reading with their child more enjoyable, but to also promote language and other cognitive skills. I will be giving a copy of *Bookworm Babies* to all the young families in my practice."

— **Mark A. Blumenthal, M.D.**
Fellow of the American Academy of Pediatrics
Associate Chairman of Pediatrics at Newton-Wellesley Hospital
School Physician, The Rivers School

"Parents of young children who love books and read early are often asked how they taught this value and skill to their children. The answer so often from these parents is "nothing!" Actually, parents may have quite naturally done many things, such as talk to their young child even before their child could respond or read signs to their child in the grocery store or show their child the items on the shopping list. They may also have read to their child from birth in a way that was warm and joyful. In addition, they may have used effective strategies, that not only made the reading pleasurable, but also invited children into the mysterious and wonderful world of literacy.

In *Bookworm Babies*, Kimberly Aulenback and Dawn Ohanian Tringas, both parents and former teachers, have provided the encouragement some may need to jump in and read to the youngest children. They also offer a host of suggestions that will help make the most of reading good books with young children. Their guidance will be especially appreciated by adults who do not have much experience reading to young children and are looking for picture book recommendations and explicit directions for activities that will enhance story time.

When important people in a young child's life share the skill of reading along with the pleasure it provides, children cannot help but want to follow in their footsteps — increasing the chance that they will not only want to learn to read, but also love to use this skill. *Bookworm Babies* will support these important people, so they can confidently, effectively and joyfully share books with young children."

— **Jane Lannak, Ph.D.**
Director, Early Childhood Learning Laboratory at Boston University
Former Children's Librarian, San Francisco Public Library

BOOKWORM
BABIES

READ. CONVERSE. NURTURE. IMPACT.

AN EASY-TO-FOLLOW HANDBOOK DESIGNED BY TEACHERS
FOR THE PARENTS OF INFANTS, TODDLERS, AND PRESCHOOLERS

KIMBERLY ZIMMER AULENBACK
& DAWN OHANIAN TRINGAS

Seven Years Press
170 Brighton Street
Belmont, MA 02478

www.bookwormbabies.com
Bookworm Babies is available on Amazon.com.

Printed in the United States of America
Font: Century Schoolbook
Cover and Interior Illustrations: Cut felt. ©2016 Kimberly Zimmer Aulenback

First Edition: 2018
10 9 8 7 6 5 4 3 2 1

ISBN-13: 978-0692713990
ISBN-10: 0692713999

For Jim, Mark, Lexi, and my entire extraordinary and loving family. The stories that spring from your ever-evolving windows will always be my favorites.

— **D. O. T.**

For my favorite readers, Bella and Ben (My Max!), for my love, Eric, and for all those teachers who knew that I was reading a book under my desk and let it go...

— **K. Z. A.**

CONTENTS

- Introduce Previewing
- Introduce Tracking
- Recognize Letters and Words
- Observe Picture Details
- Identify Physical Features
- Identify, Colors, Patterns, and Shapes
- Integrate Actions
- Vary Your Reading
- Sing Along

written by Doreen Cronin,
illustrated by Betsy Lewin
- Introduce Previewing
- Introduce New Vocabulary
- Recognize Letters and Words
- Observe Picture Details
- Recognize Expressions and Emotions
- Consider the Concept of Cause and Effect
- Introduce the Concept of Light and Shadow
- Identify Animals
- Vary Your Reading
- Sing Along

written and illustrated by Sandra Boynton
- Recognizing Letters and Words
- Consider Differences and Similarities
- Consider the Concepts of Open and Closed
- Identify Physical Features
- Identify Colors, Patterns, and Shapes
- Practice Number Sense
- Vary Your Reading
- Sing Along

written and illustrated by Karen Katz
- Introduce Tracking
- Identify Descriptive Words (Adjectives)
- Recognize Expressions and Emotions
- Identify Physical Features
- Identify Colors, Patterns, and Shapes
- Practice Number Sense
- Vary Your Reading
- Sing Along

written by Sam McBratney,
illustrated by Anita Jeram
- Introduce Previewing
- Recognize Letters and Words
- Observe Picture Details
- Make Connections
- Identify Physical Features

A NOTE FROM THE AUTHORS

As educators and literacy consultants with a passion for books, we began reading with our own children when they were newborns still in the hospital. Like all new parents, we were exhausted, but we were excited to find our way and — yes! — share books with our infants. It helped that our friends and family brought books when they came to visit, but anyone listening at the hospital door would never have known that we were reading stories with newborns. We asked questions, thought aloud, marveled at the illustrations, and chatted about the story while we were sharing it. We were new to parenting, but we were trained to read like a teacher and that was what we were doing.

To be honest, it did not occur to us that this might be an anomaly until we visited bookstores and libraries with our children and observed the way other parents read with their young ones; or spoke with parents who were not reading with their babies because they thought they were too small. We realized quickly that while many parents knew that reading was important and should involve more than opening a book, pronouncing the words, and closing the book, few had been taught how to truly unlock the unique power within the pages of a picture book. That was when the idea for *Bookworm Babies* was born.

After years of working in schools, consulting, reading with children, and observing the positive educational effects of interacting with books, conversational book-sharing became second nature as we moved from educators to parents. Our love of reading and the desire to teach our conversational book-sharing strategies to new parents became a passion. In the time we stole from work, to-do lists, and sleep, we built a website and a social media following, all focused on sharing tips for reading aloud, circulating research, curating book recommendations, answering questions from fellow parents, and perfecting The *Bookworm Babies* Method of conversational book-sharing.

We know that cultivating behaviors of literacy from infancy will ensure that children develop a proficiency for reading that will permeate all aspects of growth, development, and life experience. Our greatest desire is to pass on a love and knowledge of conversational book-sharing to every caregiver reading with a young child.

We are glad to be on this journey with you!

Dawn and Kimberly

PLEASE NOTE

Bookworm Babies
Read. Converse. Nurture. Impact.
is a handbook that can be used
by anyone who cares for a child.
For the sake of clarity, we use the word parent.

In the 20 companion book chapters, we offer a model
for what *you might say* to begin conversations.
These are merely suggestions. Your experiences will
shape the conversations you have with your child.

Sometimes the board book version of a story differs
slightly from the original. If you find that the version
of a story you are reading does not match the text
represented in the conversation starters,
you will need to modify the suggested dialogue.

THE *BOOKWORM BABIES* METHOD

Congratulations! You have entered the dynamic world of parenting. Whether you are a first-time parent or adding to your family, you are responsible for your child's basic needs. You will provide the love, support, and stimulation necessary for your child to develop into adulthood.

Every interaction, conversation, and experience you have with your little one will shape your child into the adult he or she will eventually become. Living in an increasingly competitive and global world, you will also need to ensure that your child is prepared for future success. This process begins in infancy.

Informed parents, teachers, and literacy experts begin nurturing their children's young minds when their babies are still infants in the simplest, most natural way: they read and they talk. They share books with their babies every day, often multiple times a day. Then, they talk about the books, informally and conversationally, long before their children can respond or even fully understand the content.

Babies and Books: An Educational Advantage
The simple truth is that most babies who are read with from birth have a *significant* educational advantage over their peers who have not had consistent exposure to books. Reading aloud *and talking about books* are two of the simplest, most effective, and most enjoyable ways to positively affect all aspects of a child's early intellectual growth and development, regardless of environmental factors. Babies who are read with from birth have already been exposed to concepts related to science, engineering, math, art, and language by the time they enter school. Additionally, they have activated early and vital critical-thinking skills, such as predicting and pretending, and early literacy skills, such as letter and word recognition. This essential learning and nurturing, stemming from both the reading *and the conversations inspired by books*, is paramount to a child's future success.

Bookworm Babies: Read. Converse. Nurture. Impact.
Whether you already read with your child, you are coming to book-sharing without any experience, or you are a busy parent striving

to maximize learning while holding tight to nurturing time with your little one, you have picked up the right book. *Bookworm Babies* brings impactful conversation starters to all parents. Each informal and stimulating conversation has been specially designed by teachers not only to activate stories and inspire thinking, but also to honor essential bonding time as well. The easy-to-follow handbook format provides parents with simple and effective instructions for quickly engaging all children — even infants.

The *Bookworm Babies* Method

Many parents pick up a book and read *to* a young child. An educator will pick up a book, read *with* a young child, *and engage in conversations*. The difference in methods is profound. Teachers know that books offer a multitude of educational opportunities for engaging children beyond the content of the story. Reading text with children is only one small part of the literacy experience because stories are natural springboards for rich conversations and interactions. *Bookworm Babies* guides parents to read like a teacher, combining quality children's books with enriching, nurturing, and impactful conversations.

It is important to note that most educators do not engage in early book-sharing to teach their little ones to read. Instead, educators read aloud every day to enhance the fun, excitement, wonder, and knowledge within each and every page of a story, and to prepare their children for future educational success.

What the Experts Know About Early Reading

Today more than ever, literacy studies indicate the enormous benefits of reading with children, *from birth*. A child who is read with from early infancy develops an understanding of books and reading as an integral part of daily life: conversational, nurturing, enriching, interactive, thought-provoking, *and* fun. The Center on the Developing Child at Harvard University says,

> The early years matter because, in the first few years of life, 700 new neural connections are formed every second. Neural connections are formed through the interaction of genes and a baby's environment and experiences, especially "serve and return" interaction with adults, or what developmental researchers call contingent reciprocity. These are the connections that build brain

architecture – the foundation upon which all later
learning, behavior, and health depend.[1]

In fact, these connections are so powerful that preschool and
kindergarten teachers can typically identify students who have
been read with after only a few days in the classroom.

The National Institute for Literacy published a staggering
education statistic back in 2006: "In a study conducted of
kindergartners, those who were read to at least three times a week
as they entered kindergarten were almost twice as likely to score
in the *top-25%* of literacy tests than children who were read to less
than three times a week."[2] Imagine then, the benefits of reading
like a teacher and conversing about books from infancy. Not only is
there a positive correlation between sharing books and school
success, but failure to do so can prove detrimental to your child.
According to the American Academy of Pediatrics (AAP),

Reading aloud with young children is one of the most
effective ways to expose them to enriched language and to
encourage specific early literacy skills needed to promote
school readiness. Indeed, early, regular parent-child
reading may be an epigenetic factor associated with later
reading success. . . .. Yet, every year, more than 1 in 3
American children start kindergarten without the
language skills they need to learn to read. Reading
proficiency by the third grade is the most important
predictor of high school graduation and career success.
Approximately two-thirds of children each year in the
United States and 80% of those living below the poverty
threshold fail to develop reading proficiency by the end of
the third grade.[3]

Follow Your Pediatrician's Advice

The American Academy of Pediatrics recommends that
pediatric providers promote early literacy development for
children beginning in infancy and continuing at least until
the age of kindergarten entry by (1) advising all parents
that reading aloud with young children can enhance
parent-child relationships and prepare young minds to
learn language and early literacy skills; (2) counseling all
parents about developmentally appropriate shared-reading
activities that are enjoyable for children and their parents

and offer language-rich exposure to books, pictures, and the written word.[4]

Pediatricians *want* parents to read with their children. In fact, many pediatricians give families a new book to take home sometime between the ages of six months to five years. However, statistics indicate that many parents still do not read with their children on a daily basis. The U.S. Department of Education reported: ". . . only 55 percent of children ages 3–5 (not yet in kindergarten) were read to daily by a family member; yet studies show that reading to young children provides a *significant* educational advantage."[5]

The Benefits of Early Exposure to Stories

Your baby is learning from *every* experience. Language, visual stimulators, comfort, and safety are key factors in your child's early development. Almost from day one, your child learns to associate certain stimuli with everyday life: warm milk, diaper changes, time with you and other loved ones, and the opportunity to take in new surroundings. Babies who are read with from their first day home begin to associate reading with everyday life as well. Book-sharing becomes an essential part of a daily routine, and in turn, these young children establish a lifelong habit that will activate almost every aspect of their developing minds, from infancy through adulthood.

Reading regularly with young children also stimulates optimal patterns of brain development and strengthens parent-child relationships at a critical time in child development, which, in turn, builds language, literacy, and social-emotional skills that last a lifetime.[6]

Reading with young children using The *Bookworm Babies* Method also promotes:
- an introduction to the concepts of print-based thinking, exploration, discovery, questioning, connecting, and predicting
- exposure to new and sophisticated vocabulary
- awareness of conversational tone and inflection
- stimulation and formation of crucial synapses in both the left and right hemispheres of the brain

- exposure to new learning experiences derived from text and pictures
- increased attention span
- visual stimulation for infants
- focusing and tracking skills
- strengthening of visual thinking
- an understanding of print basics, including how to hold and open a book, and that books are read from left to right
- an eagerness to read or be read with in the future
- an understanding of predictability
- an understanding of rhythm and rhyme
- knowledge of a defined beginning, middle, and end
- a visual understanding of mathematics
- exposure to early concepts of science
- introduction to multiple art forms
- sensory-motor interaction
- imagination
- perspective
- a love of reading and books
- bonding time with an engaged adult

Children's experiences are limited to their environment. As you read, the words and pictures within the pages of a book are, quite literally, new worlds for your little one. Teach The *Bookworm Babies* Method to relatives, family friends, and other caregivers. Their voices contribute to the benefits gained with each book-sharing interaction.

Remember, every book shared, and every conversation had, makes a deposit into your child's experience and background knowledge bank. Your little one will be able to draw on these investments for the rest of his or her life.

The Benefits of Conversation

Let's focus on the conversations you have with your baby for a moment. Talking with your baby not only forges a personal bond between you and your little one, but conversation also exposes young children to all the benefits of oral language. Kidshealth.org explains:

> Believe it or not, by the time babies reach their first birthday they will have learned all the sounds needed to

speak their native language. The more stories you read aloud, the more words your child will be exposed to and the better he or she will be able to talk. Hearing words helps to build a rich network of words in a baby's brain. Kids whose parents frequently talk/read to them know more words by age two than children who have not been read to, and kids who are read to during their early years are more likely to learn to read at the right time.[7]

As early as infancy, reading and conversational book-sharing contribute to crucial oral language acquisition. As children grow, hearing stories bolsters print literacy. Research confirms that: "It is through their repeated, responsive, language-rich interactions with their babies that parents have a lasting impact on their baby's brain development. This early exposure to language-rich interactions forms the basis of Language Nutrition."[8]

The *Bookworm Babies* Method of conversing about topics appropriate for a child's age and experience is crucial to enhancing a reading experience and to impacting a child's young mind. The conversations spark meaningful interactions between reader and text, teach children to wonder about what they are reading, encourage critical thinking beyond the words in a story, inspire games and songs, remind children that books are vehicles for personal and/or shared enjoyment, and offer relevant information.

Consider the concept of enhanced vocabulary acquisition, for example. Teachers know that within the pages of many children's books are words and phrases not commonly found in everyday conversations — especially the kind of conversations adults often have with very young children. In the context of well-written stories, vocabulary is presented situationally so that a relatable scenario makes sense even if some word choices are unfamiliar. Sharing stories each day exposes your child to these new, and often sophisticated, vocabulary words. The follow-up conversations, however, provide a deeper understanding of selected words and phrases, as well as their context. Repetition of these words and phrases through conversation not only promotes a varied vocabulary, but also builds the foundation for an advanced level of oral language acquisition, development, and understanding.

Getting Started Early with Infants

At first, reading with your newborn or infant will be straightforward. Simply read aloud when your child is awake, either in your arms or nearby. Your infant most certainly will not look at what you are reading, or even respond, but newborns hear your voice and take in all your language stimulators. For the most part, your baby will be a captive audience.

Sometimes parents feel silly reading with a newborn. Others do not own children's books. Some parents wonder how an infant, who may not be able to respond to a book, could possibly benefit from reading or the conversations outlined in *Bookworm Babies*. However, these same parents talk with their babies, chat during diaper changes, coo and cuddle, and/or sing lullabies. These activities do not feel silly; nor should reading a book with an infant.

As Your Child Grows

Babies who have been read with from infancy will begin to approach books just as they do other toys, as fun and enjoyable items that can be looked at, handled, played with, and shared with others. This can often lead to early book-sharing struggles.

Children very often reach for — or rip — books as you are sharing them. This is common and can make it hard to read together. Luckily, there are a number of practical strategies you can employ to engage your growing baby in a book. To begin with, if your baby wants to chew a book, let her chew it. Today, many of the stories published for children are available as a board book, a soft-book, or an indestructible book. These sturdy or soft books are ideal for babies who can grab, or rip. While your baby is chewing, exploring, or folding one book, begin a second book. Now your child has a tangible plaything, and you can continue your book-sharing time. If your little one grabs for the second book, pick up the first book again. Eventually, you will either read through a story, or reading time will simply end for that moment. You can always enjoy a story later in the day when your child is more receptive to book-sharing. Giving your child a favorite teething toy while you read is also an effective strategy. Many babies enjoy looking at books, or any kind of calm activity, while holding a toy.

Another developmental stage occurs when babies realize they have the power to open and close a book. You are reading, talking, and exploring a book with your baby, when boom, the book is closed, only to be opened right back up again, before another round of closing. The beauty of conversational book-sharing is that once your baby has been exposed to a book, you do not necessarily have to read the story straight through from beginning to end. You can simply read like a teacher and talk about whatever page your little one has opened up to — or even share just the cover.

At some point, you may find yourself reading the same book over and over again. Although this can be trying, repetition is an important learning tool for young children. In addition, you can never read too much with a child who is interested. In fact, the more you engage in a story, through the conversation starters in *Bookworm Babies*, the more your child will absorb from the reading experience.

On other days, you may spend all your reading time discussing one page of a book, or simply pointing out details of the cover. Or your little one might squirm, crawl, or walk away; that is fine, you can resume book-sharing later. Most importantly, keep reading with your little one and eventually your child will want to see what is on the next page. *The point is for your child to enjoy book-sharing every time you pick up a book.*

Choosing the Right Time to Read

Book-sharing should be an integral part of your child's daily routine. Teachers know that in just 20 minutes of reading vocabulary is expanded, ideas are formed, and perspectives are broadened. Like any other skill, practice and consistency have powerful results. When you are faced with the decision to remove something from your child's schedule, do your best to protect your child's reading time.

In an ideal world, you would be able to read whenever your little one was willing to hear a story. This means that some days books would be shared five, 10, or even 15 times. When your little one showed interest in a particular story, or simply seemed open to looking at a book, you would take the opportunity to read.

Realistically, however, scheduling will limit your book-sharing time.

One of the best aspects of reading is that you do not really need a specific time or structure. Books are small and easy to carry; therefore, you can read with your child any time — while waiting in line, sitting in the pediatrician's office, traveling in the backseat of a car, using public transportation, lying down during tummy time, or at home in a cozy chair. If possible, keep small books with you at all times so you are prepared for spontaneous book-sharing moments.

Here are a few other times you might commit to reading:
- first thing in the morning
- when your child is a captive audience — for example, in the highchair, bath, or stroller
- during mealtimes or right after eating
- before or after naptime
- at bedtime

Some parents find that their children are better able to focus while engaged in a calming activity. An effective option for these busy children is for an adult to read quietly aloud while they play. If you apply this strategy, be aware that your child may not watch you the entire time. However, it is likely that, at some point during the story, your little one will stop and look, even if only for a moment. More importantly, at all times while you read, your child will be listening. You can simply read the story or follow the conversation starters: pointing out details, engaging in a running dialogue, or singing songs. Even if you feel ignored in the process, your child will be listening and learning, and books will continue to be an important part of your daily routine. Conversely, if your child asks a question (or ten), offer an answer. If your little one decides to join in, or turn the pages of the book for you, welcome his or her participation.

Most importantly, keep reading time with your child enjoyable. If your child is eager for a lively activity, reading might create frustration, and your child could end up resenting book-sharing. Over time, this resentment might make it harder for you to share books. If reading time lasts only a few minutes and you do not finish a whole story, do not worry. It is better to enjoy a few minutes of reading together than to finish a book.

Reading with Multiple Children

Bookworm Babies is divided into two developmental sections: conversation starters for babies *without* verbal language skills and conversation starters for children *with* verbal language skills. If your schedule requires you to read with multiple children at the same time, gear your reading toward the older child(ren). Younger ones will still benefit from the conversations even if they are not able to fully engage in the content.

Books, Books, Everywhere

All young children need a bookshelf, or a book basket, of their own. As Sir Arthur Conan Doyle once said, "It is a great thing to start life with a small number of really good books which are your very own."[9] Begin building your child's book collection immediately. *Bookworm Babies* applies The *Bookworm Babies* Method of conversational book-sharing to 20 companion books. Start by locating these 20 titles. Be sure to find some of your own favorites and request books from family or friends who are looking for gift ideas.

In addition to a dedicated bookshelf, placing boxes or shelves of books in different places in your home or within your child's reach keeps books in your little one's immediate environment. Educators also love to see books by a kitchen table or highchair, in a play space, in a car, at the bottom of a stroller, and in any other place where you and your child spend the most time. The more visible your child's books are, the more you and your child are apt to read.

Reading as a Priority Over Technology

As children near school age, they will likely become increasingly attracted to such technology as television, online programming, gaming systems, and handheld devices. These will vie with books for children's attention. While these options may be something your family decides to incorporate into your routine, it is imperative that you continue to read books with your young child every single day, setting a precedent now and building a long-lasting love of reading. According to the Council on Communications and Media:

All families face issues of limited time . . . and competition for the child's interest and attention from other sources of entertainment, such as electronic media. . .. In contrast to often either passive or solitary electronic media exposure, parents reading with young children is a very personal and nurturing experience that promotes parent-child interaction, social-emotional development, and language and literacy skills during this critical period of early brain and child development.[10]

Implementing The *Bookworm Babies* Method

Reading like a teacher means maximizing the value of a book-sharing experience through conversation. Concepts related to science, mathematics, language, art, critical thinking and movement can be found within the pages of our 20 popular book recommendations. The conversational method in *Bookworm Babies* guides you to highlight these many educational features simply by changing the inflection of your voice, gesturing, counting, thinking aloud, pointing out images, singing, and asking the right questions.

Locate the 20 Companion Books

The 20 companion books in the following pages include classic favorites, international bestsellers, and popular titles. Together they provide an early reading library that can be shared with infants, toddlers, and preschoolers now and for years to come. The books were selected based on the merits of their stories, their characters, their illustrations, and their ease of accessibility. Each of the 20 books has properties, either in the text or the illustrations, that are enriching and can be accessed by children of all ages. Most are popular stories that are easy to find in libraries and local bookstores. You may already have some of the titles in your child's library. If not, pick up a few (or all 20) and begin the conversations in the following chapters.

The First Reading

Children tend to enjoy the uninterrupted nature of an initial introduction to a story. Whenever you introduce a new book, try to save most of the conversations for the second or third reading. Reading through an entire story preserves the integrity and essence of a book. In addition, exposing your child to the beginning, middle, and end of a story is important for the reading and learning experience.

The Conversation Starters

After the first reading, refer to the conversation starters in the following pages. Each book section outlines the name of a popular story to share with your child, a summary of the story, and the specific elements of the story that will take you beyond the text.

The topics and conversation starters are designed to enrich the learning associated with book-sharing through fun, interactive, and thought-provoking discussions that can be applied to classic picture books and to new favorites. *Bookworm Babies* is divided into two sections: conversation starters geared toward babies and children with *and* without verbal language skills. Pick and choose the ones you like. Add some of your own. Then, apply The *Bookworm Babies* Method of conversational book-sharing to other favorite stories.

Keep in mind that these conversation starters are not designed to be used all at once during one reading of the book. You might decide to choose one or two for each reading and select different, or favorite, options for the next reading.

As your child grows, you may find yourself posing open-ended questions to spark conversations. Be mindful that your little one may need time to think. Processing a question, studying a corresponding illustration, and formulating an answer are emerging skills for young children.

Most importantly, the conversations are meant to be just that: conversations. You are not quizzing your child on what you have read. By sharing your ideas, modeling your thinking, wondering aloud, and talking about stories, you are providing your child with an open invitation to join you in rich, organic conversation. As you model your thinking, make it clear that although you have one idea, your little one may have another thought. In this way, you encourage your child to add to the dialogue with independent ideas and questions.

A Final Note

Educators often refer to reading as an opportunity to look through a window or gaze into a mirror. When you enter into conversational book-sharing, take a moment to enjoy the window into your child's personality and the reflection of your own life experiences. Either way, you and your child will benefit from the personal connections you make every single day.

In the end, you will find that conversational book-sharing will become one of the most stimulating, enriching, educational, and enjoyable activities you and your child can engage in together.

Happy Reading!

SECTION ONE

Conversation Starters for Babies *Without* Verbal Language Skills

Although your child may be too young to truly understand every detail in the following conversation starters, there is a great deal of learning that stems from simply hearing your thoughts and any questions you pose, consider, and answer.

You might decide to use the extra pages at the back of *Bookworm Babies* to record any funny, sweet, interesting, or noteworthy moments you share while reading with your child.

The Rainbow Fish
written and illustrated by Marcus Pfister

A classic fish tale that teaches about friendship and sharing
Features: clear, conversational text; colorful, sparkling pictures

Introduce New Vocabulary

Teachers are aware that books often include vocabulary words that are unfamiliar to children. As a result, books often expose children to words they might not hear in everyday conversations. These words can give information, make a text sound more sophisticated or more like everyday speech, or help convey emotion. After you have read The Rainbow Fish and your little one is familiar with the story, you may want to explain these words: *pleased, admire, glare, emerged, alone, wise, suddenly, wavered, peculiar, delighted,* and *finally*. One way that educators explain these words is to add familiar words with similar meanings as they read. For example, on the page with the octopus, you might add the words *came out slowly* after you read the word *emerged*. You might say:

> *"Then suddenly two eyes caught him in their glare and the octopus emerged" — or came out slowly — "from the darkness." The author chose the word emerged to illustrate that the octopus did not rush out of the cave.*

Making connections to stories is a tool that educators use to encourage critical thinking. If you come across these words in other books you share, or in another setting, remind your child that you also saw them in The Rainbow Fish.

Observe Picture Details

The background details in a picture contribute useful information about what is happening in a story. Teachers often ask children to notice details in the illustrations that may not be included in the text. Spend some time on each page of <u>The Rainbow Fish</u> narrating the pictures. Tell your little one what you see and what is happening. With your finger, point out and name the background details of each picture including the bubbles, sea plants, shells, snails, crabs, clams, fish, octopus, or coral. For example, on the page where Rainbow Fish finds the cave, you might say:

Look at Rainbow Fish. He is swimming above red sea plants, a yellow and green snail, and a little green crab. He is heading toward the wise octopus to hear what she has to say. The octopus blends in with her cave. She is almost the same color as the cave walls. I can see the whites of her eyes very clearly because they are much brighter than her purple skin. I wonder if she knows that Rainbow Fish is on his way to speak with her.

While you narrate, you can incorporate what you see, predict what you think might happen, ask questions, speak from personal experience, or even make up a story to go with the picture.

Identify Physical Features

Teachers often point out familiar features of characters as they read books with young children. With your finger, point to and name the identifying characteristics of each of the sea creatures in <u>The Rainbow Fish</u>. On the page with the octopus, you might say:

Look at the wise octopus. She has eight long arms. Like a real octopus, she has little round suction cups on each arm. She uses her circular suckers to grasp objects. This octopus also has two bright eyes. I do not see her mouth.

Compare the features of any book characters with those of you and your little one. You might say:

You and I have only two arms. We do not have suction cups on our arms. We use hands and fingers to grasp our food. The octopus has suction cups on her arms because she lives in the sea. You and I live on land. We have two bright eyes as well. Here are your eyes. Here are my eyes. They are looking at you. Here is my mouth. I can use my mouth to smile at you.

Point out as many features as you can identify in each illustration.

Identify the Colors of the Rainbow

Teachers often use books to illustrate basic scientific concepts. Help your child understand the title of <u>The Rainbow Fish</u> by pointing out the colors of the rainbow found on the Rainbow Fish's body. A rainbow is formed when sunlight passes through water at a certain angle. The colors of the rainbow are always red, orange, yellow, green, blue, indigo, and violet. With your finger, point to and name the different colors on the Rainbow Fish. You might say:

> *The author, Marcus Pfister, says this is a Rainbow Fish. A real rainbow has seven colors. Let's see if we can find all seven colors on this fish. One of the colors of the rainbow is red. Look, I see a red scale on the Rainbow Fish. The next color of the rainbow is orange. He has an orange scale near his tail.*

Continue in this way until you identify all seven colors of the rainbow.

Practice Number Sense

Books provide a platform for introducing the concept of number sense and exposing children to an early visual understanding of math. Use the pages of <u>The Rainbow Fish</u> to play counting games. Pointing to the Rainbow Fish on the opening pages, you might say:

> *Look at Rainbow Fish. Some of his scales are shimmering. I wonder how many shimmering scales he has. I see one, two, three, four, five, six, seven, eight, nine, ten, eleven, twelve shimmering scales. I also see shimmering squiggly marks on his fins and tail. Let's count those too.*

As you read, count how many fish are on a page, how many bubbles you see, how many legs the octopus and the starfish have, or how many leaves are on the green sea plants. On the last page, you can count how many friends the Rainbow Fish has. Count anything else you find in the illustrations.

Teachable Moment

Often, picture books include an important message, or a moral, that resonates with young children. Teachers use these stories to reinforce specific behaviors, teach about right and wrong, or introduce a new lesson. Learning to share is a social skill important to developing friendships, and it plays a role in educational success. Reinforce the concept of sharing in <u>The</u>

Rainbow Fish by demonstrating how to share with blocks or other easy-to-grasp objects. First, bring a set of blocks or toys to your little one. If you are using blocks, you might say:

> *Look at what I have. These are blocks. Right now, I have all the blocks.*

Dole out the blocks one at a time, putting one near your child and keeping one for yourself.

> *I am sharing the blocks with you. Here is one for you, and here is one for me.*

Repeat until all the blocks have been split between you. Then, you might say:

> *I shared the blocks with you just like the Rainbow Fish shared his scales with all the other fish. Now we both have blocks.*

Look for authentic opportunities in your everyday life to point out sharing and make the connection to The Rainbow Fish.

Vary Your Reading

Reading with emphasis, or changing the inflection and tone of your voice, helps draw children into the text. While reading The Rainbow Fish, change your voice to represent the different characters. This will help give your child a clear understanding of who is speaking. For example, when the Rainbow Fish is speaking, you may decide to use a higher pitch, while the octopus might inspire you to make your voice very deep. As you vary your voice, point to the character who is speaking. Changing your facial expressions and body language can work with a change in voice to communicate a different perspective.

Sing Along

Teachers know that the repetition and rhythm in songs help young children internalize new vocabulary. Use the text and illustrations on the pages of The Rainbow Fish to spark a little song. You might sing "Somewhere Over the Rainbow", "The Rainbow Connection", or "Tiny Bubbles". Include any other songs or rhymes that are inspired by the illustrations or text.

If You Give a Mouse a Cookie
written by Laura Joffe Numeroff, illustrated by Felicia Bond

An entertaining look at the progressive consequences of
giving an energetic mouse a cookie
Features: clear, cause-and-effect text; detailed, engaging pictures

Introduce Previewing

Teachers often preview books with children to activate their
thinking before a story even begins. Start by looking at the cover of
the book. Open If You Give a Mouse a Cookie and turn it over so
that you can see the picture that spans both the front and back of
the book. Point to the title and picture. Talk about what you might
be thinking as you look at the cover. You might say:

> *This story is called If You Give a Mouse a Cookie. I wonder
> what it could be about. Look at the mouse. He is the main
> character. He is holding a cookie and he looks very happy.
> Look at these red sneakers. They look too big for the mouse.
> Let's read to find out who wears those sneakers.*

Next, point out the name of the author and illustrator. You might
say:

> *Laura Joffe Numeroff is the author. She made up the story
> and wrote down the words. The illustrator is Felicia Bond.
> She created the pictures to go along with the words.*

Introduce Tracking

Black text on a white background provides a simple platform for
helping young children learn that books have words that can be

read (or tracked) from left to right. With your index finger, point to the words on the page as you read <u>If You Give a Mouse a Cookie</u>. Start at the left and move slowly to the right and then down to the next line. You might say:

> *When I read to you, I start on the left. Then I read each word that comes next. When there are no more words to read on this line, I go down and start again on the next line. I am going to point to the words as I read them this time.*

On some pages you might point to each word as you read, and on other pages sweep your finger under the text without pausing on any particular word.

Identify Pronouns

Pronouns can be difficult for young children to grasp even though the antecedent of the pronoun seems very clear to an adult reader. Whenever you read the word *he* or *him* in <u>If You Give a Mouse a Cookie</u>, point to the little mouse. You might also add the words *the mouse* as you read the words *he* or *him*. For example, when the mouse finishes his milk, you might say:

> *When he's finished, he — the mouse — will ask for a napkin.*

This serves two purposes. First, it clarifies the words *he* and *him* used throughout the book. Second, it emphasizes the correlation between text and illustrations.

Observe Picture Details

The background details in a picture contribute useful information about what is happening in a story. Teachers often ask children to notice details in the illustrations that may not be included in the text. Spend some time on each page narrating the pictures in <u>If You Give a Mouse a Cookie</u>. Tell your little one what you see and what is happening. For example, on the first page the mouse is wearing a green backpack when he first sees the boy. The boy is offering him a cookie. On the second page, the mouse is following the boy into the house and the boy is bringing the rest of the cookies. On the next page, you might say:

> *Look, the mouse's little green backpack is on the counter, and he ate only a few bites of the cookie. He was thirsty, so the boy gave him a glass of milk, but the mouse and the boy*

> *are both looking at the glass in a funny way. Maybe they*
> *are thinking that the glass is too big for the mouse.*

Continue to point out other details in the picture, such as the cookie bag next to the toaster and the items on top of the open refrigerator. As you read on, notice what the boy carries in his back pockets. While you narrate, you can incorporate what you see, predict what you think might happen, ask questions, speak from personal experience, or even make up a story to go with the picture.

Predict and Pretend

Teachers often ask children to predict, pretend, ask questions, and think critically while they are reading. These are important tools for comprehension and advanced interaction between the reader and a book. As you read If You Give a Mouse a Cookie, expose your little one to language and interactive thoughts by modeling these tools. For example, on the first page, the mouse is walking with a backpack and the boy is reading a comic book. The boy stops reading to offer a cookie to the mouse. Looking at the picture, you might say:

> *Look at the boy. He is reading a comic book. I wonder what*
> *it says. Look at the mouse. I wonder where he is going. I*
> *wonder where he was before he got here. Maybe he was at*
> *home. I wonder what is in his little green backpack. Maybe*
> *he has a book or a snack in his little green backpack.*

Next, turn the page and point out that the boy has a baseball bat leaning against the house. Ask:

> *What do you think the boy was doing before he started*
> *reading his comic book?*

Answer this question aloud to introduce critical thinking. You might say:

> *I see a ball and a bat. I think the boy might have been*
> *playing baseball.*

While you predict and pretend, notice how prior knowledge and past experiences influence your conversation.

Consider the Concept of Cause and Effect

Teachers often use books to illustrate basic scientific concepts. Help your child understand the concept of cause and effect in If You Give a Mouse a Cookie. As you read, explain why the mouse keeps asking for something new each time the boy gives him an item. For example, on the two-page spread where the mouse asks for a straw, you might say:

> Look at the mouse. He is very small. The glass of milk the boy gives to the mouse is too big. If the mouse tried to tip the glass in order to drink the milk, it would **cause** the milk to spill. That is why the mouse asks for a straw. Now that the mouse has a straw, what **effect** will that have? He will be able to drink all the milk. Look, the mouse finished eating the cookie and drinking the milk. His mouth is dirty. This **causes** the mouse to ask for a napkin. He needs to clean his face.

Identify Colors, Patterns, and Shapes

Educators often ask young children to identify objects and patterns based on their colors and shapes. Felicia Bond's illustrations in If You Give a Mouse a Cookie are vibrant and detailed. As you share the pictures with your little one, point out various colors, shapes, and patterns. For example, in the middle of the story, there is a picture of the mouse beginning to draw with crayons on a blank sheet of paper. On the next page, you can see that he drew a picture of his family. Point to each crayon on the blank piece of paper and name the color. Then turn the page to the mouse's finished picture and point out where the crayon was used. You might say:

> The mouse is starting to draw with this green crayon. Let's turn the page and look at the picture he drew. He used the green crayon to draw these dandelion leaves. He also used the green crayon to color in the grass and draw his mother's dress. The mouse used a pink crayon to draw triangular noses, and to create the squares in the checkered pattern on his father's shirt.

You may decide to follow one object, pattern, or shape throughout the book or point out different features in each illustration.

Vary Your Reading

Reading with emphasis, or changing the inflection and tone of your voice, helps draw children into the text. In If You Give a Mouse a Cookie, the author sometimes starts a sentence on one page and then finishes it on the next page. To build anticipation, raise your voice and draw out the last word on the pages where the sentence is not finished. For example, on the page where the mouse has finished his picture and the boy is carrying all the cleaning supplies, you might read:

*"Then he'll want to hang his picture on your refrigerator. Which means he'll **neeeeeeed** . . . [turn the page] . . . Scotch tape."*

Sing Along
Teachers know that the repetition and rhythm in songs help young children internalize new vocabulary. Use the text and illustrations on the pages of <u>If You Give a Mouse a Cookie</u> to spark a little song. You might sing "Who Stole the Cookies from the Cookie Jar?" or "Hickory Dickory Dock". Include any other songs or rhymes you can think of that are inspired by the illustrations or text.

Where Is Maisy?
written and illustrated by Lucy Cousins

A lift-the-flap search for Maisy and her friends
Features: simple, short, repetitive text; bold, colorful, pictures

Introduce Previewing

Teachers often preview books with children to activate their
thinking before a story even begins. Start by looking at the cover of
the book. Point to the title and picture. Talk about what you might
be thinking as you look at the cover. You might say:

> *This story is called* Where Is Maisy?. *I wonder what it
> could be about. I wonder who Maisy is. The word* Where
> *tells me that we might be looking for someone in the story
> who is hiding. There is a picture of a mouse right here. I
> think that might be Maisy. She is standing behind a bush.
> Maybe Maisy is hiding in the story. This is a lift-the-flap
> book, which means that there will be some places in the
> pictures where we use our fingers to lift up a piece of the
> book to see another picture.*

Point out the name of the author and illustrator. You might say:

> *Lucy Cousins is the author. She made up the story and
> wrote down the words. She is also the illustrator, which
> means she created the pictures to go along with the words.*

Introduce Tracking

Black text on a white background provides a simple platform for helping young children learn that books have words that can be read (or tracked) from left to right. With your index finger, point to the words on the page as you read Where Is Maisy?. Start at the left and move slowly to the right and then down to the next line. You might say:

> When I read to you, I start on the left. Then I read each word that comes next. When there are no more words to read on this line, I go down and start again on the next line. I am going to point to the words as I read them this time.

On some pages you might point to each word as you read, and on other pages sweep your finger under the text without pausing on any particular word.

Recognize Letters and Words

Teachers use repetitive text to introduce young children to letters and words. Small words are powerful tools for emphasizing letter recognition and introducing the concept that individual letters strung together can create familiar words. Every time the word Maisy appears in Where Is Maisy?, point to it, say it, spell it, and then say it again. You might say:

> This book is called Where Is Maisy?. This is the word Maisy. The letters M-a-i-s-y spell Maisy. Look, here is the word Maisy again. Maisy begins with the capital letter M. Muh, muh, M. A capital M is a tall letter made with four slanting lines. We can find the word Maisy on each page of this book. I am going to point to the word Maisy on this page. Muh, muh, Maisy.

Point to the letters as you say each one and trace each letter with your finger.

Observe Picture Details

The background details in a picture contribute useful information about what is happening in a story. Teachers often ask children to notice details in the illustrations that may not be included in the text. Spend some time on each page of Where Is Maisy? narrating the pictures. Tell your little one what you see and what is happening. For example, when you open to the picture of the house, point out the flowers, the shrub outside the door, the mail slot, the door knob, the windows, the number five, the roof, the chimney, the bear in the window, and the bear's bow tie. You might say:

> *The brown bear is inside the house. I can see him through the window behind the green shutters. He is wearing a green shirt and a yellow bow tie. Look at the house. It is yellow with a red and orange striped roof. I see two planters — or pots — in front of the house. The orange planter has a green shrub with yellow and red flowers. The other is a brown planter with orange and blue flowers. I wonder who planted all of those flowers.*

While you narrate, you can incorporate what you see, predict what you think might happen, ask questions, speak from personal experience, or even make up a story to go with the picture.

Make Connections

Educators ask children to make connections to stories and text in order to increase comprehension. Spend some time on each page of Where Is Maisy? describing the pictures. Tell your little one what is happening and make connections. You might link the text to other books, to personal experiences, or to events in the real world. For example, on the page with the sailboat, you might say:

> *The alligator is in the sailboat. He is floating on the sea, and a bird is flying above the boat. There is a small, colorful flag at the top of the mast and the sail is yellow. Other Maisy books have the same alligator. His name is Charley. It looks like he is having a good time on the sailboat. I wonder where Charley is going on his sailboat. Maybe he is going to visit his other alligator friends. Maybe he is hunting for treasure. Perhaps we can go on a sailboat sometime. Maybe you can sail a toy boat like Charley when you take a bath.*

Making connections not only increases understanding, but also serves to honor your child's experiences, and helps your little one view stories through a personal lens.

Consider the Concepts of Open and Closed

Teachers often use books to illustrate basic scientific concepts. Lift-the-flap books are favorites of many children. If you are reading with an infant or if this is your child's first experience with a lift-the-flap book, explain that you are going to open each flap to see if Maisy is underneath. Name the flap, what is under it, and then demonstrate closing it again. For example, on the page with the donkey in the barn, you might say:

> *There are flaps on this page. They open and close. This barn door is a flap. I am going to open the door to see if Maisy is inside. Maisy is not here. There is a donkey inside the barn! Now I am going to close the door. Goodbye, donkey. Now the flap is closed.*

As soon as your little one can manipulate the flaps in <u>Where Is Maisy?</u>, let him open and close the windows, doors, tree leaves, and boat sails as many times as he wishes. If your child is opening and closing the flaps over and over again, resist the urge to turn the page. Let your little one experiment with his new-found dexterity and ability to manipulate objects. As your child opens the flap, narrate what he is doing. You might say:

> *You opened the door. You closed the door. What is behind the door? A donkey is behind the door. Open. Close. There is the donkey again. Hi, donkey. Open. Close. There are the donkey's ears. You opened the door again. Can you close it? You closed it.*

Practice Number Sense

Books provide a platform for introducing the concept of number sense and exposing children to an early visual understanding of math. Use the pages of <u>Where Is Maisy?</u> to play counting games. For example, on the last page, you might say:

> *Look at the brown planter next to the blue door. It has a green plant growing inside it. I am going to count each of the leaves on the plant. I see one, two, three, four, five, six, seven, eight, nine green leaves on the plant. I also see two flowers on the blue door. Each flower has yellow petals and a red center. Now I am going to count the yellow petals on those flowers. I see one, two, three, four, five yellow petals on each of the flowers. That means that there are ten yellow petals all together.*

As you read, you can count whiskers, flowers, stripes, doorknobs, apples, and anything else you might see in the illustrations.

Vary Your Reading

Reading with emphasis, or changing the inflection and tone of your voice, helps draw children into the text. Repetitive phrases can be used to build anticipation. Almost every page of <u>Where Is Maisy?</u> begins with "Is Maisy in the. . . ." As you read, raise your voice and draw out the last word. Then pause for a second or two before you state the place where Maisy might be found. For example, you might read the page with the house like this:

> "*Is Maisy in **theeee*** . . . [pause for a moment and point to the house] *house?"*

Changing your facial expressions and body language can work with a change in voice to communicate a different perspective.

Sing Along

Teachers know that the repetition and rhythm in songs help young children internalize new vocabulary. Use the text and illustrations on the pages of <u>Where Is Maisy?</u> to spark a little song. You might sing "Where Is Thumbkin?", "Open Them, Shut Them", "Row, Row, Row Your Boat" on the page with the boat, or "Apples and Bananas" on the page with the apple tree. Include any other songs or rhymes you can think of that are inspired by the illustrations or text.

Chicka Chicka Boom Boom
written by Bill Martin Jr. and John Archambault, illustrated by Lois Ehlert

A classic chant starring the letters of the alphabet
A shorter version can be found in the board book Chicka Chicka ABC
Features: fun, rhyming text; bright, bold pictures

Recognize Letters and Words

Teachers use repetitive text to introduce young children to letters and words. Small words are powerful tools for emphasizing letter recognition and introducing the concept that individual letters strung together can create familiar words. The first and last two-page spreads of Chicka Chicka Boom Boom showcase all the uppercase and lowercase letters of the alphabet. Use these pages to spell out familiar words to your little one. With your finger, point to specific letters and name each one, including the sound each letter makes. For example, when you point to the letter *T,* you might say:

> *Look, this is the letter* T. *Tuh, tuh,* T.

Then string the letters together to make a familiar word. You might say:

> *We can use the letter* T *to spell the word* toes. T-o-e-s *are the letters we use to spell* toes.

Point to your little one's toes. Next, point to the letters that spell out your child's name, siblings' names, or the words *mommy, daddy, bottle,* or *baby.* Spell any other words you use often in your household.

Recognize Rhyming Words

Teachers know that there is a correlation between recognizing rhymes and reading readiness. Each page in <u>Chicka Chicka Boom Boom</u> includes at least one rhyme. After you finish a page or verse that rhymes, repeat the words that rhyme. Then, list additional words that rhyme. For example, on the first page, you might read:

> *"A told B and B told C, 'I'll meet you at the top of the coconut tree.'"*

Then, say:

> *On this page the letters* B, C, *and the word* tree *all rhyme. They all have the same* eee *sound at the end. I wonder if I can think of other words that rhyme with* B, C *and* tree? *I know:* see, key, bee, *and* knee *also rhyme with* B, C, *and* tree. *They all have the same* eee *sound at the end, like* B, C, *and* tree.

Make Connections

Educators ask children to make connections to stories and text in order to increase comprehension. Spend some time on each page of <u>Chicka Chicka Boom Boom</u> describing the pictures. Tell your little one what is happening and make connections. You might link the text to other books, to personal experiences, or to events in the real world. For example, during the second half of the story, some of the letters have special features. On the page with the "skinned-knee D and stubbed-toe E and patched-up F," you might say:

> *Look at the letter* F. *The letter* F *has a bandage. Sometimes when you get hurt, we give you a bandage, too. The letter* F *must have gotten hurt when all the letters fell to the ground. The bandage is green. Your bandages are different colors. When I was little, I sometimes had bandages because I scraped my knees playing outside.*

Making connections not only increases understanding, but also serves to honor your child's experiences, and helps your little one view stories through a personal lens.

Consider Differences and Similarities

Teachers know that a basic understanding of comparisons is important for organizing ideas. Use Lois Ehlert's illustrations to highlight differences and similarities in <u>Chicka Chicka Boom Boom</u>. Notice that some letters are changed or singled out in the second half of the book. Some of the letters even have special features. For example, the letter *P* is described as having a black eye and the letter *P* in the illustration is drawn with a dark black circle. Flip back and forth between the letter *P* at the beginning of the story and the letter *P* toward the end of the story. Begin on the page with L, M, N, O, and P coming to the tree. You might say:

> *Look at the letter* P *on this page. It has a tall line connected to a curved line. There is a white circle in its center. The letter* P *is to the right of the tree, next to the letters L, M, N and O.*

Next, turn to the page where P, Q, R, S and T are at the base of the tree. You might say:

> *Now look at the letter* P *on this page. It is still a tall line connected to a curved line, but it looks different. On this page, the letter* P *has a black eye, so there is a black circle in the middle of the curved line. I notice that the letter* P *is still by the tree, but it is on the left side now. The* P *is also next to different letters.*

Next, turn to the two-page spread at the beginning or at the end of the story. Many of the books you read with your little one will be printed with both uppercase and lowercase letters. Pointing out this difference will help your little one to recognize both forms of the letters. You might say:

> *There are two different ways to write letters — uppercase and lowercase. Uppercase letters are used to begin sentences and names. This is an uppercase* A. *Right next to the uppercase* A *is a lowercase* a. *They are both the letter* A, *but they are written differently. The uppercase* A *is tall with straight lines. The lowercase* a *is smaller with a curved line.*

As you read, point out any other similarities and differences you find in the story.

Consider the Concept of Cause and Effect

Teachers often use books to illustrate basic scientific concepts. Help your child understand cause and effect by pointing to the tree in every picture of <u>Chicka Chicka Boom Boom</u>. As the letters climb up into the tree, it begins to bend. You might say:

> *Look what is happening to the tree; it is starting to lean because the letters are climbing up onto the branches. The letters must be heavier than the tree. The letters are* **causing** *the tree to lean. I wonder what will happen as*

*more letters climb onto the tree. I wonder what **effect** too many letters will have on the tree. It may bend all the way over to the ground! Let's see what happens. Chicka Chicka Boom Boom! All the letters fell out of the tree because it bent over so low.*

Identify Physical Features

Teachers often point out familiar features of characters as they read books with young children. With your finger, point to and name the identifying characteristics of each of the letters in Chicka Chicka Boom Boom. In the second half of the book, the letters receive human characteristics, like skinned-knee D, stubbed-toe E, and loose-tooth T. Point to the corresponding body parts on your child as you read about knees, toes, eyes, and teeth. When you find D and E, you might say:

This is skinned-knee D. I see a yellow bandage. Here are your knees. This is stubbed-toe E, whose toe is a little swollen. Let's point to your toes. Here they are.

When you find T, you might say:

This is loose-tooth T. I see a tooth hanging down. You have a tooth, too. Here it is, in your mouth.

(You may have to point to your own teeth if your little one does not have any yet.) Point out as many features as you can identify in each illustration.

Identify Colors, Patterns, and Shapes

Educators often ask young children to identify objects and patterns based on their colors and shapes. Lois Ehlert, the illustrator of Chicka Chicka Boom Boom, uses blocks of bright colors in her illustrations. As you share the pictures with your little one, point out various colors, shapes, and patterns found on the trees, coconuts, backgrounds, and borders. For example, on the first page, you might say:

These are the letters A, B, and C. The A is orange, the B is red, and the C is purple. Look at the tree. The tree has a dark brown trunk and leaves that are two different shades of green. It also has two brown coconuts. They are round. Look, the border on this page is orange with round, pink polka dots.

You may decide to follow one object, pattern, or shape throughout the book or point out different features in each illustration.

Vary Your Reading

Reading with emphasis, or changing the inflection and tone of your voice, helps draw children into the text. Young children love songs and chants, and Chicka Chicka Boom Boom lends itself well to a rhythmic reading. As you read the text, try to keep a chanting beat. You might even clap, snap, or tap the beat gently as you recite the words. You may also decide to pause at the end of the second line of each rhyme before reading the last word. For example, you might read:

> *"A told B, and B told C, 'I'll meet you at the top of the coconut . . .* [pause] *tree.'"*

Changing your facial expressions and body language can work with a change in voice to communicate a different perspective.

Sing Along

Teachers know that the repetition and rhythm in songs help young children internalize new vocabulary. Use the end pages of Chicka Chicka Boom Boom to sing the ABC song with your little one. Point to the uppercase and lowercase letters as you sing. Sing the ABC song in as many languages as you know. Include any other songs or rhymes you can think of that are inspired by the illustrations or text.

BIG Little
written and illustrated by Leslie Patricelli

An exploration into the differences between big and little
Features: simple, short, repetitive text; colorful, cute pictures

Recognize Letters and Words

Teachers use repetitive text to introduce young children to letters and words. Small words are powerful tools for emphasizing letter recognition and introducing the concept that individual letters strung together can create familiar words. Every time the word BIG appears in <u>BIG Little</u>, point to it, say it, spell it, and then say it again. You might say:

> *This book is called* <u>BIG Little</u>. *This is the word* BIG. *The letters* b-i-g *spell* BIG. *Look, here is the word* BIG *again.* BIG *begins with the letter* B. *Buh, buh,* B. *A capital* B *is a tall letter with one long line and two rounded lines. We can find the word* BIG *on each page of this book. I am going to point to the word* BIG *on this page. Buh, buh,* BIG.

Point to the letters as you say each one and trace each letter with your finger.

Observe Picture Details

The background details in a picture contribute useful information about what is happening in a story. Teachers often ask children to notice details in the illustrations that may not be included in the text. Spend some time on each page of <u>BIG Little</u> narrating the pictures. Tell your little one what you see and what is happening.

For example, on the page with the elephant and the mice, you might say:

> *The little boy is riding the big elephant. He is smiling, and so is the elephant. They must be happy. Look at the elephant's long trunk and big ears. I bet it would be fun to ride an elephant. I wonder where you can ride an elephant around here. Look at this picture: the boy is looking through a mouse hole. He sees three little mice. Look at their little ears, their little round noses, and their tails. Mice sometimes make a squeaking sound.*

While you narrate, you can incorporate what you see, predict what you think might happen, ask questions, speak from personal experience, or even make up a story to go with the picture.

Consider the Concept of Big and Little

Teachers often use books to illustrate basic scientific concepts. Every picture in <u>BIG Little</u> emphasizes the differences between items that are big and those that are little. Though the objects in the pictures are different sizes, they are not as profoundly different as objects can be in real life. For example, the elephant in the picture is only a little bit larger than the mice in the picture, whereas an actual elephant is many times larger than an actual mouse. To further emphasize the concept of big and little, use objects in your home or in your neighborhood to illustrate the differences between objects that are big and those that are little. You might stand up and show how big you are next to your little one after you finish reading the page that says, "Grownups are BIG. Babies are little." You might say:

> *Look, I am a grown up; I am big. You are a baby; you are little. One day you will be big, just like me.*

Find other objects to continue the big and little game. For example, you might show your little one a big round ball and compare it with a small frozen pea, or while on a walk, point to a tree and then to a flower.

Identify Physical Features

Teachers often point out familiar features of characters as they read books with young children. With your finger, point to and name the identifying characteristics of the boy in <u>BIG Little</u>. On the first two-page spread, point out all his features, including his tuft of hair, his eyes, nose, mouth, ears, rosy cheeks, diaper, arms, hands, fingers, legs, and toes. To emphasize the theme of the story, be sure to note that the little boy's head is bigger than his toes. You might say:

> Look at the little boy. He has a round head. He head is the biggest part of his body. Look, here are his toes. His toes look little compared to his head. See how tiny they are? Your head is bigger than your little toes, too. These are your little toes.

Point out as many features as you can identify in each illustration.

Identify Colors, Patterns, and Shapes

Educators often ask young children to identify objects and patterns based on their colors and shapes. Leslie Patricelli, the author and illustrator of <u>BIG Little</u>, creates bright, bold images. As you share the pictures with your little one, point out various colors, shapes, and patterns, including the lattice pattern on the elephant's blanket, the waves in the lake, and the icing on the cake. For example, on the page comparing ladies with ladybugs, you might say:

> The lady's shirt is red with round, black polka dots. Her eyes are round, too. Her skirt is a darker red than her shirt, and her shoes and her lips are red, too. Look, under the lady is a shadow that is orange. Her hair is also orange. The background color on this page is yellow.

You may decide to follow one object, pattern, or shape throughout the book or point out different features in each illustration.

Practice Number Sense

Books provide a platform for introducing the concept of number sense and exposing children to an early visual understanding of math. Use the pages of <u>BIG Little</u> to play counting games. For example, on the page with the ladybugs, you might say:

> The boy is looking at ladybugs with his magnifying glass. There is one big ladybug under the glass. That ladybug has three black spots: one, two, three. There are four smaller ladybugs to the right of the magnifying glass: one, two, three, four. That means there are five ladybugs all together because four plus one is five.

As you read, count the number of mice you see, the wheels on the truck and on the tricycle, the ladybugs, the candles on the cake, the windows on the boat, the ducks in the bathtub, and the number of big or little items in the book. Count anything else you find in the illustrations.

Vary Your Reading

Reading with emphasis, or changing the inflection and tone of your voice, helps draw children into the text. While you are reading <u>BIG Little</u>, vary your voice each time you read the words *BIG* and *little*. For example, lower and extend your voice in a booming way for the word *BIG*, and use a higher, sweeter voice for the word *little*. Changing your facial expressions and body language can work with a change in voice to communicate a different perspective.

Sing Along

Teachers know that the repetition and rhythm in songs help young children internalize new vocabulary. Use the text and illustrations on the pages of <u>BIG Little</u> to spark a little song. You might sing "I'm a Little Teapot", "Head, Shoulders, Knees, and Toes", or "Hickory Dickory Dock" on the page with the mice, "Row, Row, Row Your Boat" on the page with the boat, or "The Wheels on the Bus" on the page with the bus. Include any other songs or rhymes you can think of that are inspired by the illustrations or text.

Don't Let the Pigeon Drive the Bus!
written and illustrated by Mo Willems

A pigeon's desperate attempt to get the reader to let him drive a bus
Features: clear, conversationally typeset; Caldecott Honor Book

Recognize Letters and Words

Teachers use repetitive text to introduce young children to letters
and words. Small words are powerful tools for emphasizing letter
recognition and introducing the concept that individual letters
strung together can create familiar words. Every time the word
bus appears in Don't Let the Pigeon Drive the Bus!, point to it, say
it, spell it, and then say it again. You might say:

> *This book is called* Don't Let the Pigeon Drive the Bus!.
> *This is the word* bus. *The letters* b-u-s *spell* bus. *Look, here
> is the word* bus *again.* Bus *begins with the letter* B. *Buh,
> buh,* B. *The lowercase letter* b *has a tall straight line and
> one rounded line. We can find the word* bus *on many pages
> of this book. I am going to point to the word* bus *on this
> page. The pigeon wants to drive the* bus. *Buh, buh,* bus.

Point to the letters as you say each one and trace each letter with
your finger.

Recognize Conversation

Teachers are aware that understanding the conversational nature
of a story is an important reading skill for very young children.
The bus driver in Don't Let the Pigeon Drive the Bus! speaks
directly to the reader. The pigeon who stars in the story also

speaks directly to the reader throughout the book, as if he is having a conversation. Point out the bus driver on the title page as you read his instructions. Then point to the bus driver's words inside the speech bubble. Explain that the words in the bubble are being spoken by the person to whom the bubble is pointing. You might say:

> See this shape with a point? It is called a speech bubble. Part of the speech bubble is pointing to the bus driver. That means that he is the one saying the words inside the bubble. He is saying, "Don't let the pigeon drive the bus!" Whenever you see a speech bubble, it means someone is saying something. People in books often take turns speaking, just like in real life. In this book, the bus driver and the pigeon are talking to you.

Whenever the pigeon asks to drive the bus, you might answer *No!* before continuing to the pigeon's next response or question.

Observe Picture Details

The background details in a picture contribute useful information about what is happening in a story. Teachers often ask children to notice details in the illustrations that may not be included in the text. Spend some time narrating the pictures on each page of Don't Let the Pigeon Drive the Bus!. Tell your little one what you see and what is happening. For example, on the last page, the pigeon turns his attention to a red truck. Find the first image of the large, red truck. You might say:

> Look at the tire of this truck. It has grooves around it to help the tire grip the ground. In the center of the tire is a hub cap. It covers the bolts that secure the wheel to the axle. I see one of the truck's lights. When it is dark outside, the driver will turn on the lights. This part, on the front of the truck, is called a bumper. I also see a side step. The driver steps on this platform to get into the truck. I wonder if the pigeon has ever ridden in a truck.

Then, turn the page and point out the same features on the smaller truck. While you narrate, you can incorporate what you see, predict what you think might happen, ask questions, speak from personal experience, or even make up a story to go with the picture. As an extension to observing the details of the truck in the book, point out any trucks you see in real life. Name parts of the truck that are the same as the details you noticed on the truck the pigeon is dreaming about in the story.

Recognize Expressions and Emotions

Illustrators often vary a character's expressions or body language in order to convey a particular emotion. In <u>Don't Let the Pigeon Drive the Bus!</u>, the pigeon's eyes, mouth, and body language are very expressive. Explain to your little one that the reader can tell what the pigeon is feeling by looking carefully at how his eyes and body change in each picture. For example, on the page where the pigeon says, "Pigeon at the wheel!", you might say:

> *The pigeon is imagining himself driving the bus. He looks excited! I can tell that he is excited because his eye is wide open, and his wings are up in the air with movement lines next to them. He also has one leg in the air like he is jumping or dancing a bit, and his mouth is open.*

As you read, mimic the expressions of the characters. You might say:

> *This is how I look when I am excited like the pigeon* [express excitement].

Predict and Pretend

Teachers often ask children to predict, pretend, ask questions, and think critically while they are reading. These are important tools for comprehension and advanced interaction between the reader and a book. As you read <u>Don't Let the Pigeon Drive the Bus!</u>, expose your little one to language and interactive thoughts by modeling these tools. For example, after reading the opening instructions from the bus driver, you might say:

> *The bus driver has to leave for a little while. I wonder where he is going. Maybe he is going to have lunch. I wonder why he does not want the pigeon to drive the bus.*

On the end pages, when the pigeon is dreaming about driving the truck, you might say:

> *Boy, that pigeon really wanted to drive the bus. He was willing to do just about anything! He must really love buses, but I think he loves trucks too. Maybe he likes all big vehicles. I wonder if he has actually ever driven a bus before, or if he has only dreamed about it.*

While you predict and pretend, notice how prior knowledge and past experiences influence your conversation. You might also tell your child about something you dreamed about doing when you were a child.

Identify Physical Features

Teachers often point out familiar features of characters as they read books with young children. With your finger, point to and name the identifying characteristics of the pigeon in all his various moods and positions in <u>Don't Let the Pigeon Drive the Bus!</u>. Looking at the front cover, you might say:

> *Look at the pigeon. He looks very innocent. Look at his eye. It is wide open, and he is looking at you. His other eye must be on the other side of his head where we cannot see it. Look at the pigeon's wing. He has it folded neatly next to his body. Look at the pigeon's beak. It is yellow. These are his two legs. He is standing very still.*

Point out as many features as you can identify in each illustration.

Practice Number Sense

Books provide a platform for introducing the concept of number sense and exposing children to an early visual understanding of math. Use the pages of <u>Don't Let the Pigeon Drive the Bus!</u> to play counting games. For example, on the first page, you might say:

> *The pigeon has two legs: one, two. He also has two feet: one, two. He has three toes on each foot: one, two, three. Here are your two legs and your two feet. Here are your five toes: one, two, three, four, five. You have more toes on your foot than the pigeon does. He also has two wings and two eyes, but we can see only one of his eyes.*

As you read, count the feathers as the pigeon yells to drive the bus, the number of times you see the pigeon's eye, or the number of words in each speech bubble. On the end pages, count the buses and the trucks. Then count the wheels, the windows, and all the different positions the pigeon is in as he dreams about driving — or anything else you can find in the illustrations.

Integrate Actions

Teachers often use movement to enhance a book-sharing experience. Movement can also help active children access books. While you read <u>Don't Let the Pigeon Drive the Bus!</u>, help your child understand the correlation between text and actions. First, point to the pigeon in each illustration. Then, describe what the pigeon is doing. For example, throughout the story the pigeon is sitting, standing, bending over, whispering, running, lying down, having a tantrum, walking, and standing still. Act out these motions for your little one. On the page where the pigeon says, "I'll go first!", you might say:

> *Look, the pigeon is racing to the bus. He wants to be the first one there. I can tell that he is running fast because his wings are pumping, and his legs are off the ground. There are movement lines around his body and a zigzag on the ground beneath him. He must really want to play "Drive the Bus." This is how I look when I am running fast.* [Pump your arms and run in place.]

As you read, demonstrate other actions and movements shown in the illustrations.

Vary Your Reading

Reading with emphasis, or changing the inflection and tone of your voice, helps draw children into the text. While reading Don't Let the Pigeon Drive the Bus!, emphasize passages with question marks or exclamation points by adjusting your voice and tone. You can also use your voice to highlight the pigeon's emotions. For example, the pigeon is pleading with you by the end of the story. Use variations in your voice to portray the pigeon's urgency as you read aloud. Changing your facial expressions and body language can work with a change in voice to communicate a different perspective.

Sing Along

Teachers know that the repetition and rhythm in songs help young children internalize new vocabulary. Use the text and illustrations on the pages of Don't Let the Pigeon Drive the Bus! to spark a little song. You might sing "The Wheels on the Bus", "Little Red Wagon", or "Down by the Station". Include any other songs or rhymes you can think of that are inspired by the illustrations or text.

Daddy Kisses
written by Anne Gutman, illustrated by Georg Hallensleben

A loving look at daddy animals kissing their babies
Features: clear, repetitive text; soft, painted illustrations

Introduce Previewing

Teachers often preview books with children to activate their thinking before a story even begins. Start by looking at the cover of the book. Point to the title and picture. Talk about what you might be thinking as you look at the cover. You might say:

> *This story is called* Daddy Kisses. *I wonder what it could be about. The word* Daddy *tells me there will probably be a daddy in the story. There is a picture of a lion right here. He is standing with a baby lion. That is another clue that a daddy will be in this story, and probably a baby too. It looks like the daddy lion is kissing the baby lion on the head — a daddy kiss — just like the title.*

Point out the name of the author and illustrator. You might say:

> *Anne Gutman is the author. She made up the story and wrote down the words. Georg Hallensleben is the illustrator. He created the pictures to go with the words.*

Recognize Letters and Words

Teachers use repetitive text to introduce young children to letters and words. Small words are powerful tools for emphasizing letter recognition and introducing the concept that individual letters strung together can create familiar words. Every time the word *kiss* appears in <u>Daddy Kisses</u>, point to it, say it, spell it, and then say it again. Point to the individual letters as you say each one. You might say:

> *This book is called <u>Daddy Kisses</u>. This is the word* kiss. *The letters* k-i-s-s *spell* kiss. *Look, here is the word* kiss *again.* Kiss *begins with the letter* K. *Kuh, kuh,* K. *The lowercase letter* k *has a long straight line and two smaller straight lines that stick out to the side. We can find the word* kiss *on many pages of this book. I am going to point to the word* kiss *on this page. Kuh, kuh,* kiss.

Point to the letters as you say each one and trace each letter with your finger.

Consider Differences and Similarities

Teachers know that a basic understanding of comparisons is important for organizing ideas. Use the illustrations to highlight differences and similarities in <u>Daddy Kisses</u>. On each page, point out the two animals and explain a difference and a similarity. For example, on the page with the lions, you might say:

> *Look, both of the animals on this page are lions. The lions look different, though. The daddy lion has a mane. A mane is the longer fur around a lion's face. The baby lion does not have a mane yet.*

On the page with the squirrels, you might say:

> *Look at the daddy squirrel and his little pup. The daddy squirrel is bigger, but they both have the same color fur, black eyes, four paws, white bellies, and a long tail.*

On the page with the man and the boy, you might say:

> *Here is a picture of a man and his son. The man is bigger than his son, but they both have dark hair and similar skin color. They are both human.*

Tell your child that even though she is smaller than her parents now, someday she will be grownup too. As you read, point out any other similarities and differences you find in the story.

Identify Physical Features

Teachers often point out familiar features of characters as they read books with young children. Each daddy animal in <u>Daddy Kisses</u> gives his little one a kiss on a different body part. With your finger, point to and name each animal's body part in the illustrations. Then point out the corresponding body part on your child and give her a kiss too. For example, on the page with the daddy bunny and the baby bunny, you might say:

> *Look at the bunnies. The daddy bunny is kissing his baby bunny on the ear. This is your ear. I am going to give it a gentle kiss too. The bunnies also have black eyes, pink noses, soft fur, and white cottony tails.*

Point out as many features as you can identify in each illustration.

Identify Animals

To help build vocabulary and expose your little one to animals and their features, name each animal in <u>Daddy Kisses</u>. As you turn the pages, identify each animal, point out any distinguishing features, make the animal's sound, and reinforce the differing names of the adult and the offspring. You might explain:

> *There are often different names for adult and immature – or baby – animals, including humans. I am called an adult and you are called a child.*

On the page with the frogs, you might say:

> *This is a green daddy frog. His baby is called a froglet. The frog and the froglet look alike. Their legs are bent so that they can jump. They also have padded fingers for gripping and bright yellow eyes. Frogs make a "ribbit ribbit" sound.*

Identify Colors, Patterns, and Shapes

Educators often ask young children to identify objects and patterns based on their colors and shapes. Georg Hallensleben's illustrations in <u>Daddy Kisses</u> are filled with warm, muted tones interspersed with bursts of bright colors. As you share the pictures with your little one, point out various colors, shapes, and patterns, including the fur on the animals, the color of their eyes, and the background colors. For example, on the page with the giraffes, you might say:

> *The giraffes are orange with brown spots. Each of the spots is a different shape. They are standing in a field of green grass. I can see dark green trees behind the giraffes. There are mountains in the background. The mountains are dark blue. The sky above the mountains is a lighter blue.*

You may decide to follow one object, pattern, or shape throughout the book or point out different features in each illustration.

Practice Number Sense

Books provide a platform for introducing the concept of number sense and exposing children to an early visual understanding of math. Use the pages of <u>Daddy Kisses</u> to play counting games. On the page with the wolves, you might say:

> *Look at the daddy wolf. He has two ears: one, two. The wolf pup also has two ears: one, two. That means that there are four ears on this page because two plus two equals four. The daddy wolf has four legs: one, two, three, four. The wolf pup also has four legs, but we can only see these two. The other two are on the other side of his body.*

As you read, count spots, trees, flowers, fingers, toes, paws, tails, eyes, the words on each page, and anything else you can find in the illustrations.

Vary Your Reading

Reading with emphasis, or changing the inflection and tone of your voice, helps draw children into the text. While you are reading <u>Daddy Kisses</u>, change your voice each time you read the body part a daddy is kissing. For example, lower your voice when reading "*Daddy squirrel gives his pup a kiss on the . . .*" and raise your voice to read "*paw.*" Changing your facial expressions and body language can work with a change in voice to communicate a different perspective.

Sing Along

Teachers know that the repetition and rhythm in songs help young children internalize new vocabulary. Use the text and illustrations on the pages of <u>Daddy Kisses</u> to spark a little song. On the page with the bunny, you might sing "Here Comes Peter Cottontail", "Little Peter Rabbit", or "Do Your Ears Hang Low?". On the page with the frogs, you might sing "Five Little Speckled Frogs". Include any other songs or rhymes you can think of that are inspired by the illustrations or text.

I Love You Through and Through

written by Bernadette Rossetti-Shustak,
illustrated by Caroline Jayne Church

An up-close and loving look at the personality traits
and body parts of one little boy and his teddy bear
Features: large, simple text; bold, colorful, engaging pictures

Introduce Previewing

Teachers often preview books with children to activate their
thinking before a story even begins. Start by looking at the cover of
the book. Point to the title and picture. Talk about what you might
be thinking as you look at the cover. You might say:

> *This story is called <u>I Love You Through and Through</u>. I
> wonder what it could be about. The word* Love *tells me
> there might be some people who love each other in the story.
> There is a picture of a teddy bear right here, so I think that
> is a clue that a teddy bear will be in this story. The boy is
> holding the teddy bear up in the air. The boy and the teddy
> bear are both smiling. I wonder if they love each other.*

Point out the name of the author and the illustrator. You might
say:

> *Bernadette Rossetti-Shustak is the author. She made up the
> story and wrote down the words. Caroline Jayne Church is
> the illustrator. She created the pictures to go along with the
> words.*

Introduce Tracking

Black text on a colored background provides a simple platform for helping young children learn that books have words that can be read (or tracked) from left to right. With your index finger, point to the words on the page as you read I Love You Through and Through. Start at the left and move slowly to the right and then down to the next line. You might say:

> When I read to you, I start on the left. Then I read each word that comes next. When there are no more words to read on this line, I go down and start again on the next line. I am going to point to the words as I read them this time.

On some pages you might point to each word as you read, and on other pages sweep your finger under the text without pausing on any particular word.

Recognize Letters and Words

Teachers use repetitive text to introduce young children to letters and words. Small words are powerful tools for emphasizing letter recognition and introducing the concept that individual letters strung together can create familiar words. Each time the word *love* appears in I Love You Through and Through, point to it, say it, spell it, and then say it again. You might say:

> This book is called *I Love You Through and Through*. *This is the word* love. *The letters* l-o-v-e *spell* love. *Look, here is the word* love *again.* Love *begins with the letter* L. *Luh, luh,* L. *The lowercase letter* l *is a tall straight line. We can find the word* love *on many pages of this book. I am going to point to the word* love *on this page. Luh, luh,* love.

Point to the letters as you say each one and trace each letter with your finger.

Recognize Expressions and Emotions

Illustrators often vary a character's expressions or body language in order to convey a particular emotion. The characters in I Love You Through and Through are very expressive. In each illustration, the teddy bear either mimics the little boy or reacts to one of the boy's many moods or situations. Point out the *boy* in each picture and tell your little one what the *boy* is doing, what expressions he is making, or how he might be feeling. Then explain what expression the *teddy bear* is making and what the *teddy bear* might be feeling. For example, on the page where the boy is in the high chair, you might say:

> *Look at this picture. The little boy is upset. The food bowl is on his head and his spoon is empty! It looks like he might be crying and yelling at the same time. Now look at his bear. The bear has his hands up by his face. He looks like he is worried. I think he is thinking, "Oh, no! My friend is upset."*

As you read, mimic the expressions of the characters. You might say:

> *This is how I look when I am worried like the bear* [express worry], *but this is how I look when I am happy again* [express happiness].

Make Connections

Educators ask children to make connections to stories and text in order to increase comprehension. Spend some time narrating the pictures on each page of I Love You Through and Through. Tell your little one what is happening and make connections. You might link the text to other books, to personal experiences, or to events in the real world. For example, on the page where the little boy is taking a bath, you might say:

> *The little boy is taking a bath with his teddy bear. He is raising his arms into the air. Look, I can raise my arms, too. Sometimes we raise our arms when we are happy. I have seen you raise your arms when you are happy. I think the boy is happy that he is in the bath with his bubbles and his teddy bear. When I was little I liked to pop the bubbles in the bath. Sometimes you have bubbles in your bath, too.*

Making connections not only increases understanding, but also serves to honor your child's experiences, and helps your little one view stories through a personal lens.

Identify Physical Features

Teachers often point out familiar features of characters as they read books with young children. With your finger, point to and name the boy's features and the features of the bear in I Love You Through and Through. For example, on the first page, you might say:

> *Look, these are the boy's toes. He has one, two, three, four, five toes on each foot. Look at your toes. You have five toes*

on each foot, too. Look at the bear. He does not have any toes. He has round paws. They both have two ears. The illustrator drew their ears the same. These are your ears. They look just like my ears. Their eyes are the same, too. Their eyes are both round dots. I am looking at you with my eyes. I can blink my eyes. Both the bear and the boy have rosy red cheeks. These are your cheeks.

Point out as many features as you can identify in each illustration.

Identify Colors, Patterns, and Shapes

Educators often ask young children to identify objects and patterns based on their colors and shapes. Caroline Jayne Church, the illustrator of I Love You Through and Through, uses bright, bold colors in her pictures — sometimes solid, sometimes in stripes — and a few patterns, designs, and shapes. As you share the illustrations with your little one, point out and name different colors, designs, shapes, and also the background colors and papers in each illustration. For example, on the first page of the story, you might say:

Look at what the boy is wearing. He is wearing a striped shirt. First there are orange stripes, then red ones. His shorts are light purple. The boy and the bear both have rosy red cheeks. It looks like they are sitting on a black line. Maybe the line is their shadow. The words on the page are also black. The whole page is colored deep purple. Both the bear and the boy have eyes that look like black circles.

You may decide to follow one object, pattern, or shape throughout the book or point out different features in each illustration.

Practice Number Sense

Books provide a platform for introducing the concept of number sense and exposing children to an early visual understanding of math. Use the pages of I Love You Through and Through to play counting games. For example, on the page where the boy cries, count his tears. Pointing with your finger, you might say:

Look at the boy. He is very sad. He is crying. I can see tears in the air near his eyes. Let's count his tears. He has one, two, three, four big tears and one little tear. That means that he has five tears all together because four plus one equals five.

As you read, count fingers, toes, ears, rosy cheeks, hands, feet, bubbles, and anything else you can find in the illustrations.

Vary Your Reading

Reading with emphasis, or changing the inflection and tone of your voice, helps draw children into the text. While reading I Love You Through and Through, consider emphasizing words to match what they are trying to convey. For example, when you read "*I love your happy side*" let your voice go up for the words *happy* or *happy side*. When saying "*and your sad side,*" let your voice drop for the words *sad* or *sad side*. Read each emotion in a way that suggests a specific feeling. Smile when reading a positive word or scowl when reading a negative word. Changing your facial expressions and body language can work with a change in voice to communicate a different perspective.

Sing Along

Teachers know that the repetition and rhythm in songs help young children internalize new vocabulary. Use the text and illustrations on the pages of I Love You Through and Through to spark a little song. You might sing "You Are My Sunshine", "Head, Shoulders, Knees, and Toes", "You Are the Apple of My Eye", or "The Hokey Pokey". Include any other songs or rhymes you can think of that are inspired by the illustrations or text.

Brown Bear, Brown Bear, What Do You See?
written by Bill Martin Jr., illustrated by Eric Carle

A question-and-answer classic identifying animals and colors
Features: simple, repetitive text; classic Eric Carle illustrations

Introduce Previewing

Teachers often preview books with children to activate their
thinking before a story even begins. Start by looking at the cover of
the book. Point to the title and picture. Talk about what you might
be thinking as you look at the cover. You might say:

> *This story is called <u>Brown Bear, Brown Bear, What Do You
> See?</u>. I wonder what it could be about. The word* Bear *tells
> me there will probably be a bear in the story. There is a
> picture of a bear right here, so I think that is another clue
> that a bear will be in this story. The bear is walking. I
> wonder where he is going. I wonder if he is going to see
> some other animals while he is walking.*

Point out the name of the author and illustrator. You might say:

> *Bill Martin Jr. is the author. He made up the story and
> wrote down the words. Eric Carle is the illustrator. He
> created the pictures to go along with the words.*

Introduce Tracking

Black text on a white background provides a simple platform for
helping young children learn that books have words that can be
read (or tracked) from left to right. With your index finger, point to

the words on the page as you read <u>Brown Bear, Brown Bear, What Do You See?</u>. Start at the left and move slowly to the right and then down to the next line. You might say:

> *When I read to you, I start on the left. Then I read each word that comes next. When there are no more words to read on this line, I go down and start again on the next line. I am going to point to the words as I read them this time.*

On some pages you might point to each word as you read, and on other pages sweep your finger under the text without pausing on any particular word.

Recognize Letters and Words

Teachers use repetitive text to introduce young children to letters and words. Small words are powerful tools for emphasizing letter recognition and introducing the concept that individual letters strung together can create familiar words. Every time the word *see* appears in <u>Brown Bear, Brown Bear, What Do You See?</u>, point to it, say it, spell it, and then say it again. Point to the individual letters as you say each one. You might say:

> *This book is called <u>Brown Bear, Brown Bear, What Do You See?</u>. This is the word* see. *The letters* s-e-e *spell* see. *Look, here is the word* see *again.* See *begins with the letter S. Sss, sss, S. The letter S is a curvy line. We can find the word* see *on many pages of this book. I am going to point to the word* see *on this page. Sss, sss,* see.

Point to the letters as you say each one and trace each letter with your finger.

Observe Picture Details

The background details in a picture contribute useful information about what is happening in a story. Teachers often ask children to notice details in the illustrations that may not be included in the text. Spend some time narrating the pictures on each page of <u>Brown Bear, Brown Bear, What Do You See?</u>. Many of the animals in the illustrations are in motion. For example, the bear and duck are walking, the dog is running, the bird is flying, the horse is eating, the sheep, teacher, and children are looking at the reader, and the goldfish is swimming. Tell your little one what you see and what is happening. On the page with the dog, you might say:

> *Look at the white dog. I think the dog is running. I can tell*
> *because its front paw is lifted, and its tongue is hanging out*
> *of its mouth. When I run, I lift my leg a little higher than*
> *when I am walking. I wonder where the dog is going.*

While you narrate, you can incorporate what you see, predict what
you think might happen, ask questions, speak from personal
experience, or even make up a story to go with the picture.

Identify Physical Features

Teachers often point out familiar features of characters as they
read books with young children. With your finger, point out the
identifying features of each animal in <u>Brown Bear, Brown Bear,
What Do You See?</u>. For example, the duck has an orange beak that
is slightly open, brown eyes, a tail, and two webbed feet. Point out
as many features as you can identify. On the page with the cat,
you might say:

> *Look at the purple cat. I see two bright green eyes and two*
> *pointy ears. I can also see long black whiskers, four paws,*
> *and a long tail. Look at the purple cat's nose; it looks like a*
> *little pink triangle. Its tongue is also pink. The cat has*
> *lifted its left front paw to lick it clean.*

Point out as many features as you can identify in each illustration.

Identify Colors, Patterns, and Shapes

Educators often ask young children to identify objects and patterns
based on their colors and shapes. Eric Carle is a master of using
bright, bold colors in his illustrations. As you share the pictures
with your little one, point out various colors, shapes, and patterns
found in <u>Brown Bear, Brown Bear, What Do You See?</u>. For
example, on the page with the red bird, you might say:

> *Look at this bird with the bright red body. Its wings and*
> *tail are red too, but the wings also have some brown*
> *feathers. The red bird has a black face and a bright yellow*
> *beak. The beak is made with two long triangular shapes.*
> *The red bird is flying on a white background. The words on*
> *the page are black.*

You may decide to follow one object, pattern, or shape throughout
the book or point out different features in each illustration.

Integrate Actions

Teachers often use movement to enhance a book-sharing experience. Movement can also help active children access books. While you read <u>Brown Bear, Brown Bear, What Do You See?</u>, help your child understand the correlation between text and actions. First, point to the animals in each illustration. Then, describe what the animals are doing. For example, the bear, the dog, and the duck are walking, the bird is flying, the fish is swimming, the cat is licking her paw, and the sheep and the teacher are looking at you. Act out the motions for your little one. On the page with the blue horse, you might say:

> *The blue horse is bending down to the ground, searching for something to eat. The horse uses its mouth and its teeth to chew food, just like we do. Look at my mouth. This is what my mouth looks like when I am chewing. We do not bend down to eat our food like the horse does. We bring the food up to our mouths. Sometimes we use a fork or a spoon, and sometimes we use our hands.*

As you read, demonstrate other actions and movements shown in the illustrations.

Vary Your Reading

Reading with emphasis, or changing the inflection and tone of your voice, helps draw children into the text. Use the question-and-answer pattern in <u>Brown Bear, Brown Bear, What Do You See?</u> to vary your voice to represent each animal. For example, you might use your regular voice to ask, *"Brown Bear, Brown Bear, what do you see?"* and then a deep voice for *"I see a red bird looking at me."* Changing your facial expressions and body language can work with a change in voice to communicate a different perspective.

Sing Along

Teachers know that the repetition and rhythm in songs help young children internalize new vocabulary. Use the text and illustrations on the pages of <u>Brown Bear, Brown Bear, What Do You See?</u> to spark a little song. When you have the brown bear page open, sing "The Bear Went Over the Mountain". When you have the black sheep page open, sing "Baa, Baa, Black Sheep, Have You Any Wool?". On the page with the green frog, you might sing "Five Little Speckled Frogs". Include any other songs or rhymes you can think of that are inspired by the illustrations or text.

Click, Clack, Moo: Cows That Type
written by Doreen Cronin, illustrated by Betsy Lewin

An entertaining exchange between Farmer Brown and his
dissatisfied cows, complete with hens and a mediating duck
Features: big, bold type; Caldecott Honor Book

Introduce Previewing

Teachers often preview books with children to activate their
thinking before a story even begins. Open <u>Click, Clack, Moo: Cows
That Type</u> so that you can see the picture that spans both the front
and back of the book. Point to the title and picture. Talk about
what you might be thinking as you look at the cover. You might
say:

> *This story is called <u>Click, Clack, Moo: Cows That Type</u>. I
> see that there are some cows, hens, and a duck in the
> picture. These are farm animals. I wonder if this story
> might take place on a farm. I see something unusual in the
> cover picture. It is a machine called a typewriter. People
> used this kind of machine to type letters and stories before
> there were computers. Some people still do. You put the
> paper into the machine, then press the buttons — or keys —
> and a letter in the machine presses ink onto the paper. I
> notice that one of the cows has his foot in the air over the
> keys of the typewriter while the others watch him type. I
> wonder what kind of note a cow would want to type. Maybe
> the hen and the duck are helping the cows in the story.*

Point out the name of the author and illustrator. You might say:

Doreen Cronin is the author. She made up the story and wrote down the words. Betsy Lewin is the illustrator. She created the pictures to go along with the words.

Introduce New Vocabulary

Teachers are aware that books often include vocabulary words that may be unfamiliar to children because they do not name something you can point to on the page. These words can give information, make a text sound more sophisticated or more like everyday speech, or help convey emotion. After you have read Click, Clack, Moo: Cows That Type and your little one is familiar with the story, you may want to explain these words: *believe, impossible, sincerely, growing, impatient, furious, demand, neutral, ultimatum, emergency, gathered, snoop, exchange, decided,* and *boring.* One way that educators explain these words is to add familiar words with similar meanings as they read. For example, on the page where the cows hold their emergency meeting, you might add the words *secretly listen* after you read the word *snoop.* You might say:

> *"All the animals gathered around the barn to snoop," — or secretly listen — "but none of them could understand Moo." I think the author chose the word snoop instead of listen to show that the other animals were not supposed to be there.*

In addition, you may want to discuss the following (possibly) unfamiliar items as you read the story: *typewriter, electric blankets, stool, buckets,* and *udders.* Making connections to stories is a tool that educators use to encourage critical thinking. If you come across these words or items in other books you share, or in another setting, remind your child that you also saw them in Click Clack, Moo: Cows That Type.

Recognize Letters and Words

Teachers use repetitive text to introduce young children to letters and words. Small words are powerful tools for emphasizing letter recognition and introducing the concept that individual letters strung together can create familiar words. Every time the word *moo* appears in Click, Clack, Moo: Cows That Type, point to it, say it, spell it, and then say it again. You might say:

> *This book is called Click, Clack, Moo: Cows That Type. This is the word moo. The letters m-o-o spell moo. Look, here is the word moo again. Moo begins with the letter M. Mmm, mmm, M. A capital M is a letter made with four*

slanting lines. We can find the word Moo *on many pages of this book. I am going to point to the word* moo *on this page. Mmm, mmm,* moo.

Point to the letters as you say each one and trace each letter with your finger.

Observe Picture Details

The background details in a picture contribute useful information about what is happening in a story. Teachers often ask children to notice details in the illustrations that may not be included in the text. Spend some time on each page of <u>Click, Clack, Moo: Cows That Type</u> narrating the pictures. Tell your little one what you see and what is happening. You might focus on the barn, the farmer, the birds, the cows, the hens, the typewriters, the trees, and the ducks, or pause to focus on one image in any given illustration. Then, spend a few moments pointing out defining characteristics. For example, on the page where Farmer Brown cries, "No milk today!", you might say:

> *Look at the cows. They are all gathered around the typewriter. The cows have black spots. I can point to their hoofed feet, their pink noses, their two ears, their two eyes, and their two horns. These are dairy cows. I can tell because I can see that the cows have pink udders. The udders are where the cows store their milk. I wonder when the farmer will milk the cows.*

While you narrate, you can incorporate what you see, predict what you think might happen, ask questions, speak from personal experience, or even make up a story to go with the picture.

Recognize Expressions and Emotions

Illustrators often vary a character's expressions or body language in order to convey a particular emotion. The characters in <u>Click, Clack, Moo: Cows That Type</u> are very expressive. Point out the animals and the farmer in each picture and tell your little one what they are doing, what expressions they are making, or how they might be feeling. On the first page, you might say:

> *Look at the farmer. The farmer looks angry on this page. His eyebrows are slanted, and his mouth is turned down. He hears the cows typing in the red barn. Farmer Brown's cows usually do not type, so he is probably confused.*

As you read, mimic the expressions of the characters. You might say:

> *This is how I look when I am angry like the farmer* [express anger], *but this is how I look when I am happy again* [express happiness].

Consider the Concept of Cause and Effect

Teachers often use books to illustrate basic scientific concepts. Help your child understand the concept of cause and effect in Click, Clack, Moo: Cows That Type by explaining why the animals are making demands. For example, on the page where Farmer Brown first sees the note from the cows, you might say:

> *Look at the note from the cows. The barn is cold. That* **causes** *the cows to be cold. The cows are asking for blankets to keep them warm.*

Then look at the page with the note about the hens. You might say:

> *The hens are cold in the barn, too. This* **causes** *the hens to ask for blankets to keep them warm.*

Turn to the page with the cows and hens sleeping in the barn with their electric blankets. You might say:

> *The electric blankets have an* **effect** *on the cows and hens. They are sleeping peacefully now. They are nice and warm in the barn.*

Finally, look at the pages with the ducks. You might say:

> *The ducks are bored in the pond. This* **causes** *the ducks to ask for a diving board. A diving board would make the pond more fun. Look, here is the duck on the last page. The duck is diving into the water and this* **causes** *the water to rise in a big splash.*

Consider the Concept of Light and Shadow

Teachers often use books to illustrate basic scientific concepts. The illustrations in Click, Clack, Moo: Cows That Type include shadows made with watercolors. Explain to your little one that a shadow is formed when an object blocks light. When light cannot pass through an object, a shadow appears where the light does not reach. Shadows are sometimes long and sometimes short, depending on the position of the light. For example, on the page where Farmer Brown first sees the note from the cows, point out the shadow of his hat and face. You might say:

Look at this. The sun is shining behind Farmer Brown. His hat is bright yellow from the sun. The sun is casting a shadow on the note and on the wall. This is Farmer Brown's shadow. It is the same shape as Farmer Brown's hat and face. I see the straw here, his nose here, and his beard here. The nail that is holding up the note also has a shadow. The shadows cover some of the words, but we can still read what the note says.

On the next page, point out that although you cannot see Farmer Brown standing there in the picture, you can tell by the shadow that he is still there. You might say:

Farmer Brown was standing here reading the note, and we saw his shadow. This is his shadow again. We can tell what he is doing with his body by what his shadow is doing. I can see the straw from his hat, his arms, and his legs. I am going to guess that he is upset, because his fists are up, and he looks like his legs are stomping or jumping.

As you read, point out other illustrations that have shadows.

Identify Animals

To help build vocabulary and expose your little one to animals and their features, name each animal in <u>Click, Clack, Moo: Cows That Type</u>. As you turn the pages, identify each animal, point out any distinguishing features, make the animal's sound, and tell your little one what the animal provides for the farmer. For example, on the page where one hen is holding the closed sign, you might say:

Look at these birds. They are called hens. Hens make the sound "bok, bok, bok." This flock of hens lives on the farm with Farmer Brown and the cows. Farmer Brown raises hens because hens lay eggs. He takes the eggs from the hens. He most likely keeps some eggs and sells some eggs. People can probably buy Farmer Brown's eggs. The eggs we have in our home came from hens, too. I can see that each of the hens has a sharp beak. Hens have pointed beaks so that they can peck food from the ground. The food Farmer Brown feeds the hens gives them the nutrition they need to lay their eggs.

Vary Your Reading

Reading with emphasis, or changing the inflection and tone of your voice, helps draw children into the text. Sometimes text lends itself to a special rhythm or provides an opportunity to emphasize certain phrases. For example, some lines in <u>Click, Clack, Moo: Cows That Type</u> have similar length and can be read with the same cadence: "*Cows that **type!** Hens on **strike!**"* You can also read lines that are repeated throughout the book with the same emphasis each time. For example, lower and extend your voice for the word *moo* each time it is written: *"Click, clack, mooooo. Clickety, clack, mooooo."* Changing your facial expressions and body language can work with a change in voice to communicate a different perspective.

Sing Along

Teachers know that the repetition and rhythm in songs help young children internalize new vocabulary. Use the text and illustrations on the pages of <u>Click, Clack, Moo: Cows That Type</u> to spark a little song. When you see the farmer, sing "The Farmer in the Dell" or "Old McDonald Had a Farm". Include any other songs or rhymes you can think of that are inspired by the illustrations or text.

Moo, Baa, La La La!
written and illustrated by Sandra Boynton

A fun look at well-known animals and their sounds
Features: classic, Sandra Boynton rhyming text;
whimsical animals on solid backgrounds

Recognize Letters and Words

Teachers use repetitive text to introduce young children to letters
and words. Small words are powerful tools for emphasizing letter
recognition and introducing the concept that individual letters
strung together can create familiar words. Every time the word *La*
appears in <u>Moo, Baa, La La La!</u>, point to it, say it, spell it, and
then say it again. You might say:

> *This book is called* <u>Moo, Baa, La La La!</u>*. This is the word*
> La. *The letters* L-a *spell* La. *Look, here is the word* La
> *again.* La *begins with the letter* L. *Luh, luh,* La.

Point to the letters as you say each one and trace each letter with
your finger.

Consider Differences and Similarities

Teachers know that a basic understanding of comparisons is
important for organizing ideas. Use Sandra Boynton's illustrations
to highlight differences and similarities in <u>Moo, Baa, La La La!</u>.
There are two pages of pigs in <u>Moo, Baa, La La La!</u>. On one page,
the pigs are dancing, and on the other, they are simply saying
oink. Turn to the page with the dancing pigs. Point to the shirts,
bow ties, jackets, belts, pants, and canes. Next, turn to the

following page and point out differences and similarities between the two sets of pigs. You might say:

> *Look at these dancing pigs. They are wearing striped pants and holding canes. The pigs are singing "la la la!" and are standing on two legs. Now look on the next page. These are pigs, too. They are similar because they have the same nose, the same ears, and the same hooves. They are also different. These pigs are not dancing. They are standing on four legs and they are not wearing any clothes.*

As you read, point out any other similarities and differences you find in the story.

Consider the Concepts of Open and Closed

Teachers often use books to illustrate basic scientific concepts. The illustrations in <u>Moo, Baa, La La La!</u> introduce the concepts of open and closed. Starting with the front cover, point to the sheep and the pigs. Tell your child that the pigs and the sheep have their eyes wide open, but their mouths are closed. You might say:

> *Look at the sheep. Its eyes are wide open. Look at the sheep's mouth. It is closed. Look at the pigs. They have their eyes wide open, too. They are also smiling, and their mouths are closed as well. The cow's eyes are wide open, but we cannot see its mouth.*

Next, open the book and point to each animal's open mouth in the illustrations. Tell your child that the animals have their mouths open on these pages because they are speaking. For example, on the first page, you might say:

> *Look at the cow. Its eyes are still open, just not as wide. The cow's mouth is open because it is saying "moooooo."*

Turn to the last page of the book. On the last page all the animals have their eyes open, but they have closed mouths once again. You might say:

> *All the animals have their mouths closed again. They are waiting quietly. They want you to open your mouth and make a sound.*

Open and close your mouth to show the difference.

Identify Physical Features

Teachers often point out familiar features of characters as they read books with young children. The animals in <u>Moo, Baa, La La La!</u> are drawn with prominent details and features. With your finger, point out and name the different characteristics of each animal, including hooves, webbed feet, paws, udders, ears, eyes, mouths, horns, tails, noses, whiskers, manes, and beaks. For example, on the page with the rhinoceroses and the little dogs, you might say:

> Look at the two large, grey animals on this page. They are called rhinoceroses. Sometimes we call them rhinos. Rhinos have very large feet, pointy ears, round bodies, and little tails. They also have two horns on their noses. Their mouths are snorting and snuffing, and their eyes look a little bit angry. The rhinos look like they are angry at the dogs. I notice that all three of the dogs are little, but they do not look exactly the same.

Point out as many features as you can identify in each illustration.

Identify Colors, Patterns, and Shapes

Educators often ask young children to identify objects and patterns based on their colors and shapes. Sandra Boynton uses blocks of color in her illustrations. In fact, each page of Moo, Baa, La La La! has a different background color. As you share the pictures with your little one, point out various colors, shapes, and patterns. For example, on the first page of the book, you might say:

> This page is colored lime green. I can see a white cow with black spots. Each of the spots is a different shape. The cow has a pink udder and a pink nose. It also has a grey eyelid that is shaped almost like a half circle. The words on the page are written in black.

You may decide to follow one object, pattern, or shape throughout the book, or point out different features in each illustration.

Practice Number Sense

Books provide a platform for introducing the concept of number sense and exposing children to an early visual understanding of math. Use the pages of Moo, Baa, La La La! to play counting games. For example, on the front cover, you might say:

> There are one, two, three windows on the cover of this book. I am going to count the animals in the windows. I see one cow, one sheep, and one, two, three pigs. That means there are one, two, three, four, five animals on the cover. Each animal has two eyes. I am going to count their eyes: one,

two, three, four, five, six, seven, eight, nine, ten eyes. I can also count by twos: two, four, six, eight, ten eyes again.
As you read, count spots on the cow, bow ties on the pigs, rhinoceroses' horns, dog collars, cats, any of the animals on the last page, or anything else you find in the illustrations.

Vary Your Reading
Reading with emphasis, or changing the inflection and tone of your voice, helps draw children into the text. Use the shape and size of the animals and words in Moo, Baa, La La La! to determine how much volume and emphasis to put into each animal sound. For example, you might read large animal sounds that are in bold lettering, such as *BOW WOW WOW,* with loud, dramatic emphasis, and small animal sounds written in a smaller, thinner font, such as *ruff ruff ruff,* with a quieter voice. You can also repeat sounds over and over to emphasize each animal's sound. Instead of one *baa,* you might say:
A sheep makes the sound "baa, baa, baa, baa, baa."
In addition, you can make each page more playful by adding other sound details. For example, after reading *"Rhinoceroses snort and snuff,"* you can actually snort and snuff. Changing your facial expressions and body language can work with a change in voice to communicate a different perspective.

Sing Along
Teachers know that the repetition and rhythm in songs help young children internalize new vocabulary. Use the text and illustrations in Moo, Baa, La La La! to spark a little song. When you have the sheep page open, sing "Baa Baa Black Sheep" or "Old MacDonald Had a Farm". The page with the dogs can lead to "How Much Is That Doggie in the Window?" or "BINGO". Include any other songs or rhymes you can think of that are inspired by the illustrations or text.

Counting Kisses
written and illustrated by Karen Katz

A loving family helps their tired baby to bed with sweet kisses
Features: descending numbers and simple adjectives; colorful, patterned pictures

Introduce Tracking
Large text on a solid background provides a simple platform for helping babies learn that books have words that can be read (or tracked) from left to right. With your index finger, point to the words on the pages of <u>Counting Kisses</u> as you read them, starting at the left and moving slowly to the right and then down to the next line. You might say:

> *When I read to you, I start on the left. Then, I read each word that comes next. When there are no more words to read on this line, I go down and start again on the next line. I am going to point to the words as I read them this time.*

On some pages you might point to each word as you read, and on other pages sweep your finger under the text without pausing on any particular word.

Identify Descriptive Words (Adjectives)
Teachers know the importance of exposing young children to descriptive words that add detail to a sentence. In <u>Counting Kisses</u>, each kiss is preceded by an adjective. Point out the adjectives on each page and mimic the kinds of descriptive kisses

the baby is receiving. For example, on the page with the number ten, you might say:

> Look at this page. The mommy is giving her baby **ten little kisses** on her **teeny tiny** toes. I am going to give you **little kisses** on your **teeny tiny** toes, too.

On the page with the number seven, you might say:

> The grandmother is giving the baby **seven loud** kisses on a **pretty** belly button. I am going to give you a **loud** kiss too.

On the page with the number five, you might say:

> The baby's big sister is giving the baby **five quick** kisses on her **itty bitty** nose. I am going to give you a **quick** kiss, too.

Recognize Expressions and Emotions

Illustrators often vary a character's expressions or body language in order to convey a particular emotion. The baby in <u>Counting Kisses</u> is very expressive. Explain how you can tell what the baby is feeling by looking carefully at the illustrations. Looking at the first page of the book, you might say:

> Look at the tired baby. She looks very sad. She is crying, and her eyes are closed. She is resting her head on her mommy's shoulder. The mommy is snuggling the baby to try to make her feel better. I think she needs to take a nap.

As you read, mimic the expressions of the characters. You might say:

> This is how I look when I am sad like the baby [express sadness], but this is how I look when I am happy again [express happiness].

Identify Physical Features

Teachers often point out familiar features of characters as they read books with young children. With your finger, point to and name the body parts highlighted in <u>Counting Kisses</u>. Compare the character features with those of you and your little one. For example, on the page with ten little kisses, you might say:

> Look at the mommy in this picture. She is holding her baby's feet in her hands. These are your hands. The mommy is using her lips to kiss the baby's teeny tiny toes. Look, these are your lips. The mommy has her eyes closed. Look at me. I am closing my eyes just like the mommy in the story. These are your teeny tiny toes. Your toes are on

your feet. The baby in the story has ten teeny tiny toes, five on each foot. Let's count your toes, too.

Point out as many features as you can identify in each illustration.

Identify Colors, Patterns, and Shapes

Educators often ask young children to identify objects and patterns based on their colors and shapes. Karen Katz uses colorful details in her illustrations. As you share the pictures in Counting Kisses with your little one, point out the colors, shapes, and patterns in the curtains, rugs, shirts, wallpaper, tablecloths, couches, chairs, and bedspreads. For example, on the last page, where the baby is sleeping, you might say:

The baby's shirt is pink with red hearts. The blanket she is sleeping under is red with white and blue flowers. The blanket also has orange and white square blocks up at the top. The sheet in her crib is blue with round, white polka dots, and the bumper is green with a pattern of white triangles.

You may decide to follow one object, pattern, or shape throughout the book or point out different features in each illustration.

Practice Number Sense

Books provide a platform for introducing the concept of number sense and exposing children to an early visual understanding of math. Each page in Counting Kisses has a number spelled out, the number itself, and a corresponding number of hearts. Point out these three ways of representing the numbers. First, point out the number, then count the hearts, and then read the word. For example, on the page that says, "seven loud kisses on a pretty belly button," you might say:

Look, this is the number 7. It is written in pink. Let's count the red hearts at the top of the page: one, two, three, four, five, six, seven red hearts. Look at these letters: s-e-v-e-n. The letters s-e-v-e-n spell the number seven. The number seven is represented in three different ways on this page.

Point out the number, count the hearts, and find the word for each of the other numbers in the story.

Vary Your Reading

Reading with emphasis, or changing the inflection and tone of your voice, helps draw children into the text. While reading Counting

<u>Kisses</u>, change your voice for the different characters and for the type of kisses the baby is receiving. For example, when the mommy gives "ten little kisses on teeny tiny toes," you may decide to use a higher pitch. "Eight squishy kisses on chubby, yummy knees" might inspire you to make your voice deeper. Changing your facial expressions and body language can work with a change in voice to communicate a different perspective.

Sing Along

Teachers know that the repetition and rhythm in songs help young children internalize new vocabulary. Use the text and illustrations on the pages of <u>Counting Kisses</u> to spark a little song. When you turn to the page with the baby snug in bed, you might sing "Rock-a-bye Baby" or "Lullaby and Goodnight". Include any other songs or rhymes you can think of that are inspired by the illustrations or text.

Guess How Much I Love You
written by Sam McBratney, illustrated by Anita Jeram

A tender story about the immeasurable love between a parent and a child
Features: simple, conversational text; soft watercolors

Introduce Previewing
Teachers often preview books with children to activate their thinking before a story even begins. Start by looking at the cover of the book. Point to the title and picture. Talk about what you might be thinking as you look at the cover. You might say:

> *This story is called* Guess How Much I Love You. *I wonder what it is about. The word* Love *in the title gives me a hint. There are two hares in the picture. I like the way they are looking at each other. They look like they love each other very much. I wonder what the hares will do in the story.*

Point out the name of the author and illustrator. You might say:

> *Sam McBratney is the author. He made up the story and wrote down the words. Anita Jeram is the illustrator. She created the pictures to go along with the words.*

Recognize Letters and Words
Teachers use repetitive text to introduce young children to letters and words. Small words are powerful tools for emphasizing letter recognition and introducing the concept that individual letters strung together can create familiar words. Every time the word *Love* appears in Guess How Much I Love You, point to it, say it, spell it, and then say it again. You might say:

> *This book is called* Guess How Much I Love You. *This is the word* love. *The letters* l-o-v-e *spell* love. *Look, here is the word* love *again.* Love *begins with the letter* L. *Luh, luh,* L. *The lowercase letter* l *is a tall straight line. We can find the word* love *on many pages of this book. I am going to point to the word* love *on this page. Luh, luh,* love.

Point to the letters as you say each one and trace each letter with your finger.

Observe Picture Details

The background details in a picture contribute useful information about what is happening in a story. Teachers often ask children to notice details in the illustrations that may not be included in the text. Spend some time on each page of Guess How Much I Love You narrating the pictures. Tell your little one what you see and what is happening. Point out and name environmental details in each illustration, such as the trees, leaves, grass, fences, stones, wildflowers, mushrooms, shrubs, butterflies, insects, meadows, blue skies, and moonlight. On the page with the tree stump, you might say:

> *Look at this picture. Little Nutbrown Hare is playing on the tree stump. A tree stump is what is left of a tree after it has been cut down. I wonder who cut down the tree. Big Nutbrown Hare is standing on the soft, green grass. There are mushrooms next to the tree stump and little plants growing, too. There is a stone wall behind Big Nutbrown Hare. I can see trees in the background and little birds flying above the wall.*

While you narrate, you can incorporate what you see, predict what you think might happen, ask questions, speak from personal experience, or even make up a story to go with the picture.

Make Connections

Educators ask children to make connections to stories and text in order to increase comprehension. Spend some time on each page of Guess How Much I Love You narrating the pictures. Tell your little one what is happening and make connections. You might link the text to other books, to personal experiences, or to events in the real world. On the page where Little Nutbrown Hare says, "I love you all the way up to my toes!", you might say:

Look at Little Nutbrown Hare. He is upside down with his feet on the trunk of the tree. Little Nutbrown Hare must really love Big Nutbrown Hare, because he turned himself upside down to show how far away his toes are from his hands. I bet that made Big Nutbrown Hare feel really good. Mommies and daddies feel good when they know that their children love them. I love you very much, too, just like Little Nutbrown Hare and Big Nutbrown Hare love each other. I cannot hop as high as Big Nutbrown Hare, but I can show you I love you with snuggles. I also show you I love you by helping you fall asleep, feeding you, reading with you, and taking care of you.

Making connections not only increases understanding, but also serves to honor your child's experiences, and helps your little one view stories through a personal lens.

Identify Physical Features

Teachers often point out familiar features of characters as they read books with young children. With your finger, point out and name identifying features of Little Nutbrown Hare and Big Nutbrown Hare in <u>Guess How Much I Love You</u>. For example, the hares have long ears, furry tails, twitching noses, soft fur, long legs, three-toed feet, little eyes, light spots, and smiling mouths. On the first page, you might say:

Look at Big Nutbrown Hare. He has two long ears. They are brown on the outside and pink on the inside. He has long feet. He has only three toes on each of his feet. Big Nutbrown Hare has a brown nose and long whiskers. He also has a fluffy white tail. Little Nutbrown Hare looks just like his daddy, but his body is much smaller.

Point out as many features as you can identify in each illustration.

Integrate Actions

Teachers use movement to enhance a book-sharing experience. Movement can also help active children access books. While you read <u>Guess How Much I Love You</u>, help your child understand the correlation between text and actions. First, point to Little Nutbrown Hare and Big Nutbrown Hare in each illustration. Then, describe what the hares are doing. Act out the motions for your little one. For example, on the page that says, "I love you as high as I can reach," you might say:

*Look at Little Nutbrown Hare in this picture. He is
standing up straight and reaching way up high with his
little paws. He is telling his daddy that he loves him as
high as he can reach. Big Nutbrown Hare is standing up
straight, too. His legs are spread apart, and he is reaching
as high as he can. Little Nutbrown Hare is watching him
with his arms and his ears down. Maybe he is wishing he
had arms like his daddy. Look at me. I can reach way up
high, too. Let's raise your hands up high like Little
Nutbrown Hare and Big Nutbrown Hare.*

As you read, demonstrate other actions and movements shown in
the illustrations.

Vary Your Reading

Reading with emphasis, or changing the inflection and tone of your
voice, helps draw children into the text. While reading Guess How
Much I Love You, change your voice to represent the different
characters. This will give your child a clearer understanding of
who is speaking. For example, when Little Nutbrown Hare is
speaking, you may decide to use a higher pitch, while Big
Nutbrown Hare might inspire you to make your voice deeper. As
you vary your voice, point to the character who is speaking.
Changing your facial expressions and body language can work
with a change in voice to communicate a different perspective.

Sing Along

Teachers know that the repetition and rhythm in songs help young
children internalize new vocabulary. Use the text and illustrations
on the pages of Guess How Much I Love You to spark a little song.
You might sing "Here Comes Peter Cottontail" or "You Are My
Sunshine". At the end of the story when Little Nutbrown Hare
goes to sleep, sing "Rock-a-bye Baby" or "Lullaby and Goodnight".
Include any other songs or rhymes you can think of that are
inspired by the illustrations or text.

Mr. Brown Can Moo! Can You?
Dr. Seuss's Book of Wonderful Noises
written and illustrated by Dr. Seuss

A journey into the wonderful sounds Mr. Brown
and the reader can make together
Features: clear, rhyming text that incorporates familiar sounds;
classic Dr. Seuss illustrations

Introduce Previewing

Teachers often preview books with children to activate their
thinking before a story even begins. Start by looking at the cover of
the book. Point to the title and picture. Talk about what you might
be thinking as you look at the cover. You might say:

> *This story is called* <u>Mr. Brown Can Moo! Can You?</u>*. I
> wonder what it could be about. The name* Mr. Brown *tells
> me there is a man in the story. There is a picture of a man
> right here, and his mouth is in an O shape, like he is
> making a noise. He is standing with a cow. I wonder if Mr.
> Brown is mooing. I wonder if he can make other noises.*

Point out the name of the author and illustrator. You might say:

> *This says: "Dr. Seuss's Book of Wonderful Noises". Dr.
> Seuss is the author. He made up the story and wrote down
> the words. Dr. Seuss is also the illustrator. He created the
> pictures to go along with the words.*

Introduce Tracking

Black text on a white background provides a simple platform for helping young children learn that books have words that can be read (or tracked) from left to right. With your index finger, point to the words on the page as you read <u>Mr. Brown Can Moo! Can You?</u>. Start at the left and move slowly to the right and then down to the next line. You might say:

> *When I read to you, I start on the left. Then I read each word that comes next. When there are no more words to read on this line, I go down and start again on the next line. I am going to point to the words as I read them this time.*

On some pages you might point to each word as you read, and on other pages sweep your finger under the text without pausing on any particular word.

Recognize Letters and Words

Teachers use repetitive text to introduce young children to letters and words. Small words are powerful tools for emphasizing letter recognition and introducing the concept that individual letters strung together can create familiar words. Turn to the last two-page spread in <u>Mr. Brown</u> Can Moo! Can You?. Point to each set of words. Say each word, spell each word, and then say the word again. Be sure to point to the letters as you read and trace each letter with your finger. For example, as you point to the words *BUZZ BUZZ*, you might say:

> *Look at these two blue-green words. They say BUZZ BUZZ. B-U-Z-Z spells BUZZ. BUZZ starts with the letter B. This is the letter B. The capital letter B has one tall straight line and two rounded lines. The letter B makes a buh sound. Buh, buh, BUZZ. The words DIBBLE DIBBLE and BOOM BOOM also have Bs in them.*

Recognize Rhyming Words

Teachers know that there is a correlation between recognizing rhymes and reading readiness. Each two-page spread in <u>Mr. Brown Can Moo! Can You?</u> includes at least one rhyme. After you finish a page or verse that rhymes, repeat the words that rhyme. Then list additional words that rhyme. For example, on the first page, you might read:

"Oh, the wonderful sounds Mr. Brown can do! He can sound like a cow. He can go MOO MOO"

Then say:

On this page, the words do *and* moo *rhyme. They both have the same* ooh *sound at the end. I wonder if I can think of other words that rhyme with* do *and* moo. *I know,* boo, who, new, two *and* shoe *also rhyme with* do *and* moo. *They all have the same* ooh *sound at the end like* do *and* moo.

Observe Picture Details

The background details in a picture contribute useful information about what is happening in a story. Teachers often ask children to notice details in the illustrations that may not be included in the text. Spend some time narrating Dr. Seuss's unique illustrations on each page of <u>Mr. Brown Can Moo! Can You?</u>. Tell your little one what you see and what is happening. For example, Mr. Brown's facial expressions and body language change with every sound he makes. His eyes are always closed and near Mr. Brown's mouth are squiggly lines that reflect the sound being released. Point to Mr. Brown's face and the sounds he makes as you read. On the first page, you might say:

Look at Mr. Brown. He is saying MOO MOO. Look at his mouth. It is puckered in the shape of the ooooh sound. There are lines drawn near his mouth that show that he is mooing. The cow is looking at Mr. Brown. The cow looks happy, and a bit surprised, that Mr. Brown is saying MOO. I can tell the cow is happy and surprised because it is smiling, and its eyes are wide.

While you narrate, you can incorporate what you see, predict what you think might happen, ask questions, speak from personal experience, or even make up a story to go with the picture.

Consider Differences and Similarities

Teachers know that a basic understanding of comparisons is important for organizing ideas. Help your child conceptualize Dr. Seuss's unique versions of familiar objects by pointing out and labeling characters, animals, insects, plants, and objects in the pictures. For example, a horse or a rooster drawn by Dr. Seuss is sure to look different than a horse or a rooster in real life, or from any other toy or book your child has been exposed to before. Tell your child how Dr. Seuss's pictures differ from pictures drawn in a more realistic way. On the page that says, "KLOPP KLOPP KLOPP", you might say:

> *Dr. Seuss is the illustrator of <u>Mr. Brown Can Moo! Can You?</u>. Look at the way Dr. Seuss drew this horse. His horse is purple and has a spiky mane. The horse has a deeply swayed neck and it smiles with its eyes closed. Real horses are not purple. Most real horses have manes that are longer and necks that are straighter. Real horses do not have wide, toothless smiles.*

If possible, show your little one a picture of a real horse and point out the differences between the two images. As you read, point out any other similarities and differences you find in the story.

Identify Colors, Patterns, and Shapes

Educators often ask young children to identify objects and patterns based on their colors and shapes. Dr. Seuss's illustrations contrast bright colors against white or solid backgrounds. As you share the pictures with your little one, point out and label all the various colors, shapes, and patterns found in <u>Mr. Brown Can Moo! Can You?</u>, including details such as Mr. Brown's tie, the colors of the butterfly's wings, the different sounds on each page, and the color inside the clock. For example, on the page where Mr. Brown is buzzing, you might say:

> *Look at these two bees. They have green wings, black-and-orange striped bodies, and long, black legs. Their eyeballs look like little hearts. Both bees are wearing orange mittens and booties. Both bees have two black antennae with little round balls on top.*

You may decide to follow one object, pattern, or shape throughout the book or point out different features in each illustration.

Integrate Actions

Teachers use movement to enhance a book-sharing experience. Movement can also help active children access books. While you read <u>Mr. Brown Can Moo! Can You?</u>, help your child understand the correlation between text and actions. First, point to the animals, insects, and even inanimate objects in each illustration. Then, describe what they are doing. For example, the cow is smiling, the bees are talking to each other, the bottle is popping, the horse is walking, and the rain is falling. Act out the motions for your little one. On the page with the goldfish, you might say:

Look at these two goldfish. They are in a fishbowl. The goldfish are swimming toward each other. Their lips are going to touch. I can tell because their mouths are puckered close together. Look at my face. I am going to blow you a kiss. Now my lips are puckered, too. The water is spilling out of their fishbowl, right above their heads. They must be swimming toward each other quickly. This is what I look like when I am swimming. [Act out swimming.]

As you read, demonstrate other actions and movements shown in the illustrations.

Vary Your Reading

Reading with emphasis, or changing the inflection and tone of your voice, helps draw children into the text. Whenever you read one of the sounds in <u>Mr. Brown Can Moo! Can You?</u>, concentrate on emphasizing the words and syllables, holding the sounds a little longer than normal, using the range of your voice, reading louder or softer depending on the sound, and experimenting with your own vocal tones. For example, when you read *"BOOM BOOM BOOM Mr. Brown is a wonder,"* you might read the words *BOOM BOOM BOOM* with a stronger, more forceful tone. When you read *"whisper whisper . . . very soft very high . . . ,"* drop your voice down to a whisper. Changing your facial expressions and body language can work with a change in voice to communicate a different perspective.

Sing Along

Teachers know that the repetition and rhythm in songs help young children internalize new vocabulary. Use the text and illustrations on the pages of <u>Mr. Brown Can Moo! Can You?</u> to spark a little song. On the pages with the cow or the horse, you might sing "Old MacDonald Had a Farm". On the page where Mr. Brown says *"pop, pop, pop, pop,"* sing "Pop! Goes the Weasel". To showcase more sounds, sing "The Wheels on the Bus Go 'Round and 'Round", concentrating on the sounds on the bus. Include any other songs or rhymes you can think of that are inspired by the illustrations or text.

The Dot
written and illustrated by Peter H. Reynolds

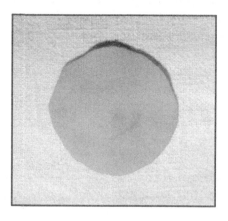

An inspiring journey from self-doubt to self-confidence
Features: hand lettered text; vibrant watercolor accents

Observe Picture Details
The background details in a picture contribute useful information about what is happening in a story. Teachers often ask children to notice details in the illustrations that may not be included in the text. Spend some time on each page of <u>The Dot</u> narrating the pictures. Tell your little one what you see and what is happening. For example, turn to the two-page spread when Vashti begins to paint a better dot than the one her teacher hung on the wall in art class. In the first image, she is sitting at a desk with her watercolors, a pencil, two different paint brushes, a bottle full of water, and several sheets of paper, each with one dot in the center. In the next picture, she has taped a larger piece of paper on the wall, moved her water jar to a stool, and has drawn several dots while experimenting with colors. Turning to the following page, you might say:

> *Look, Vashti is on the floor now. She is drawing on a much larger sheet of paper. It is big enough for her body and her dot! A little grey water container is next to the wall. I think that is a container of water because when you paint with water colors you need to wet the paints to activate them — or get them to work. You also need to swirl your paintbrush in water so that it is clean when you choose a new color.*

She has also brought two cans of paint and two large brushes to work with alongside her original watercolors. I wonder what colors are in those paint cans. I notice blue, red, and yellow in her dot, so maybe those are the colors in the cans. I think she might be using some combination of watercolors and regular paint.

Continue to point out other details in the pictures, such the materials Vashti uses, canvas sizes, and dot colors. While you narrate, you can incorporate what you see, predict what you think might happen, ask questions, speak from personal experience, or even make up a story to go with the picture.

Introduce New Vocabulary

Teachers are aware that books often include vocabulary words that are unfamiliar to children. As a result, books often expose children to words they might not hear in everyday conversations. These words can give information, make a text sound more sophisticated or more like everyday speech, or help convey emotion. After you have read <u>The Dot</u> and your little one is familiar with the story, you may want to explain these words: *gazing, swirly, glued, grabbed, jab, hmmph, discovered, experimented,* and *splashed.* One way that educators explain these words is to add familiar words with similar meanings as they read. For example, when Vashti meets the little boy at the art show, you might say:

"Vashti notices a little boy gazing" — or looking — "up at her." This page says that the little boy gazed *at Vashti. I think the author chose the word gazed instead of just saying looked or stared, so you would know that he was looking at Vashti carefully and steadily and admiring her. I am going to gaze at you, so you can see what that looks like.*

On the page with Vashti's artwork framed on the wall, you might say:

This page says that Vashti's dot was "All framed in swirly" — or curved — "gold." The author chose the word swirly to let you know that the frame was not just gold and straight. I can see the rounded and wavy parts of the frame in the picture. I also think he used the word swirly because he knows it is an adjective that kids sometimes use.

Making connections to stories is a tool that educators use to encourage critical thinking. If you come across these words in other books you share, or in another setting, remind your child that you also saw them in <u>The Dot</u>.

Consider Word Choice

Authors sometimes use idioms or common colloquial phrases to add charm and character to their text. Teachers know that while these phrases are fun to read and make sense in the context of the book, they often need to be explained to very young children. In <u>The Dot</u>, Peter H. Reynolds includes phrases such as: "glued to her chair", "a polar bear in a snowstorm", "set to work", "made quite a splash", and "I can't draw a straight line with a ruler". Explain some of these fun word choices to your little one. For example, on the page where Vashti is sitting in the classroom by herself, you might say:

> *This says that Vashti sat "glued to her chair." That sounds funny! She was not really glued to her chair! This makes me think about why the author chose the word* glued. *When you glue something, you mean for it to stick in one place. I think he chose the phrase "glued to the chair" to give you a specific idea about the way she was sitting in her chair. She was not lounging, she was not moving to get up, she was not wiggling; she was sitting very still in one spot.*

On the page where the teacher looks at Vashti's empty paper, you might say:

> *To me, this looks like a clean, empty piece of paper without a mark on it. Vashti did not draw anything at all, but the teacher tells Vashti that her all white piece of paper looks like a "polar bear in a snow storm." I wonder why she said that. Polar bears are white animals that live in cold climates. Snow is white too. So, if a polar bear was in a snowstorm, you would not really be able to see it. Everything would look white. Vashti's teacher was making a joke. I think she said it looked like a polar bear to try to make Vashti laugh a little and feel less upset because the teacher was hoping to encourage Vashti to try again. I like that the author did not just have the teacher say "you did not draw anything"; that was a good choice.*

Recognize Expressions and Emotions

Illustrators often vary a character's expressions or body language in order to convey a particular emotion. In <u>The Dot</u>, Vashti's eyes, mouth, and body language are very expressive. Her emotions are further illustrated by the watercolors that frame her in certain images. Explain to your little one that the reader can tell what Vashti is feeling by looking carefully at how her eyes and body change in each picture and what colors surround her. For example, on the page where Vashti "gives the paper a good, strong jab," you might say:

> *Vashti seems really upset in this picture. She does not think she can draw and her teacher asked her to make a mark. I can tell she is upset because the story says she jabbed her marker against the paper. A jab is much stronger than a gentle mark. I can also see she is upset because she is sitting backwards in her chair. She is not facing her paper, so she has to turn her body around to make her mark. Look at Vashti's eyes. Her eyebrows are drawn at a slant, so I know she has furrowed her brow* [show your little one a furrowed brow]. *I also noticed that Vashti is surrounded by the colors red and orange. Red is often used to illustrate anger. The red water colors seem to reflect Vashti's angry and frustrated mood.*

Next, turn to the two-page spread where all of Vashti's dots are on display at the school art show. You might say:

> *Look at Vashti now. She is holding her drawing pad in a gentle way and looking at a sculpture. Her mouth is turned up and she looks like she is happy. She is also surrounded by the color yellow. Yellow is a color often used to illustrate happiness or content. I think Vashti feels happy because people are enjoying her artwork. See, look at all the other people on the page. Vashti's art makes them feel happy. This is what my face looks like when I am smiling and happy* [show your little one your smile].

Predict and Pretend

Teachers often ask children to predict, pretend, ask questions, and think critically while they are reading. These are important tools for comprehension and advanced interaction between the reader and a book. As you read The Dot, expose your little one to language and interactive thoughts by modeling these tools. For example, on the very last page, Vashti asks the boy to sign his name after drawing a squiggly line. Looking at the picture, you might say:

Look at the boy. Vashti is asking him to sign his name. He looks like he cannot believe she wants his signature. I wonder what will happen next. I think he is going to sign his name. Maybe Vashti will hang his drawing in a fancy frame. Remember when Vashti's teacher hung her first dot in a swirly gold frame? Maybe the boy will see the frame and feel inspired to draw many kinds of squiggly lines. Then he can hang all his artwork just like Vashti did. I wonder if he will inspire someone else to draw. Or maybe they will draw a picture together. I think we will draw something together one day.

While you predict and pretend, notice how prior knowledge and past experiences influence your conversation.

Make Connections

Educators ask children to make connections to stories and text in order to increase comprehension. Spend some time on each page of The Dot narrating the pictures. Tell your little one what is happening and make connections. You might link the text to other books, to personal experiences, or to events in the real world. For example, on the page where Vashti jabs the marker onto the paper, you might say:

In this part of the story, Vashti jabs the marker onto the paper. I think she is feeling frustrated because she thinks she cannot draw. I do not think she would have jabbed the marker onto the paper if she was feeling calm. Sometimes when I am frustrated I get a bit grumpy, too, just like Vashti. I get especially frustrated when I am having trouble doing something, if I am running late, or if I drop and break what I am holding. It is very normal to feel frustrated because sometimes things are hard. We have to always remember that trying is important.

On the page where Vashti discovers that blue and yellow make green, you might say:

Vashti is mixing colors together. When you mix the color blue and the color yellow, you can make green. I loved to make green with paints when I was little. I also loved to make purple. I could make purple by mixing blue and red. Blue was my favorite color when I was young, so I loved to use it as much as I could. If I were Vashti, all my dots

*would have blue in them. I wonder what your favorite color
will be.*

Making connections not only increases understanding, but also
serves to honor your child's experiences, and helps your little one
view stories through a personal lens.

Consider Differences and Similarities

Teachers know that a basic understanding of comparisons is
important for organizing ideas. Use Peter H. Reynolds'
illustrations to highlight differences and similarities in The Dot.
On many of the pages, the background includes a dot surrounding
Vashti. These dots are different colors throughout the book. Open
to the two-page spread showing the teacher studying Vashti's
jabbed dot and then asking her to sign it. You might say:

> *Look at the illustrations on these pages. The teacher and
> Vashti's paper are drawn in black and white. I also see
> some watercolor highlights in different shades of grey and
> brown.*

Next turn the page and note the illustration of Vashti printing her
name under her first dot. You might say:

> *Now, look at the illustration on this page. It is similar, but
> there are also some differences. Vashti and the paper are
> still drawn in black and white with shades of grey, but
> there is a new color on the page. An orange dot is
> surrounding Vashti. Orange is a color that is made by
> mixing two different colors: red and yellow.*

The color of the dot surrounding Vashti changes as the story
progresses. Show your child the way the dot and Vashti look on
different pages and point out the different colors and how they
relate to Vashti's mood. You might say:

> *Vashti is almost always surrounded by a dot in the
> illustrations, but the dot is different each time. When she is
> starting to feel less frustrated the dot is orange, and when
> she is motivated to try painting, the dot changes to green. I
> think Peter H. Reynolds wants to give you a different
> feeling when he changes the color of the dot.*

Next turn to the page where the boy is drawing his line. Point out
the similarity between the multi-colored dot surrounding him, and
the multi-colored dot surrounding Vashti on the page where she
stands next to the stool and experiments with many colors. You
might say:

Look at this beautiful, colored dot around the boy. It is made up of many colors. Vashti is helping him discover what he can do. She is inspiring him. It reminds me of the dot around Vashti when she was discovering what she could do. Their dots are very similar because they are made up of many different colors. Some of the colors are the same and some are different. I have similar nice feelings when I look at both of them.

A special difference between this book and other books is that Peter H. Reynolds uses his own handwriting as the typeset. On the first page of the story, show your child the words on the page. You might say:

Look at these words; they look a little different from the words in some of the other books we read together. All the words in this book were written by the author with a pen or with a marker, instead of typed on a typewriter or computer. I wonder why he decided to do that. Maybe it was to make the words and the drawings look even more connected. I like his handwriting.

As you read, point out any other similarities and differences you find in the story. When you read other books by Peter H. Reynolds, you can remind your child about The Dot having had similar handwriting text.

Teachable Moment

Often, picture books include an important message, or a moral, that resonates with young children. Teachers use these stories to reinforce specific behaviors, teach about right and wrong, or introduce a new lesson. There are several themes in The Dot that are relevant to children and adults alike. Exploring your own creativity, bravely overcoming self-doubt, finding self-confidence, building momentum, and inspiring others are all ways to "make your mark." Talk with your little one about these themes as you read. For example, on the page where the young boy is gazing up at Vashti at the art show, you might say:

Look at this little boy. He is excited by Vashti's dots at the school art show. He is gazing up at her because he thinks she is a wonderful artist. The little boy does not know that at the beginning of the story Vashti was upset and frustrated. She did not think she could draw anything at all. Remember what her teacher said? Her teacher told her

to "just make a mark and see where it takes you." Vashti
began with one tiny dot and built momentum. That means
she kept making more and more dots in new and creative
ways. The more dots she made, the easier it became for her
to explore and create. Now she has a whole wall full of art
and feels happy and proud of herself. Vashti reminds me to
keep trying, even when something is hard at first.

As you finish the story, you might say:

The little boy was just like Vashti at the beginning of the
story. He did not think he could draw either. He was so
nervous when he was drawing a line that his hand was
shaking. His line came out all squiggly. Vashti looked at
his artwork and asked him to sign his name on the paper,
just like her teacher told her to sign her name when she
drew her first dot. Vashti has changed so much now that
she has created her dots. Instead of feeling worried about
art, she is inspiring the little boy to feel brave and make his
own mark!

Identify Colors, Patterns, and Shapes

Educators often ask young children to identify objects and patterns
based on their colors and shapes. Peter H. Reynolds' illustrations
in The Dot are vibrant and detailed. As you share the pictures
with your little one, point out various colors, shapes, and patterns.
For example, in the middle of the story, there is a two-page spread
showing Vashti's work displayed at the art show. Point to each
canvas on the wall and name the shapes you see. You might say:

Vashti has a lot of canvases on this wall of the art show.
They are different sizes and shapes. Some of her canvases
are long rectangles and some are a kind of rectangle that is
called a square. I am going to point to each of the canvases
and name the shape: square . . . rectangle . . . rectangle . . .
square . . . [etc.]. Some of the rectangles are long and
narrow. Others are wider. They are hung in different ways,
but they are all still rectangles. Look at this large rectangle.
It takes up a great deal of room on the wall. Let's look at
Vashti's dots. Dots are a shape called a circle. I am going to
point to the circles.

Continue to point to the dots on each canvas and name the colors
you see. You might say:

The dots Vashti has painted are all different colors. Let's name some of the colors of the dots we see. One of the dots is all white. Vashti painted with green and blue around the large canvas, so the middle is a white circle. This dot is yellow, this one is green and yellow, this dot is blue, and this dot is purple with green and yellow marks. Some of the dots even have designs inside of them. I am trying to decide which dot is my favorite.

You may decide to follow one object, pattern, or shape throughout the book or point out different features in each illustration.

Practice Number Sense

Books provide a platform for introducing the concept of number sense and exposing children to an early visual understanding of math. Use the pages of The Dot to play counting games. Pointing to the opening page, you might say:

Look at Vashti's classroom. There are tables and chairs in the room. I am going to count the tables: one, two, three tables. I wonder how many chairs there are. I am going to count them too: one, two, three, four, five, six, seven, and the one she is sitting on makes eight. I wonder if there are more chairs and tables in the classroom that we cannot see. I also see four items on the table where Vashti is sitting: paper, a paintbrush, a pencil, and her box of watercolors.

Next, turn to the page where Vashti opens her water color box. You might say:

Look, Vashti's watercolor box is open. Let's count how many colors are in it: one, two, three, four, five, six colors. She also has three pieces of paper: one, two, three. She still has one pencil and one paintbrush.

As you read, count how many dots are on a page, how many fingers you see, how many pieces of paper Vashti has, or how many buckets of paint are on the floor. Count anything else you and your little one can find in the illustrations.

Vary Your Reading

Reading with emphasis, or changing the inflection and tone of your voice, helps draw children into the text. While reading The Dot, change your voice to represent the different characters. This will help give your child a clear understanding of who is speaking. For example, when the teacher is speaking you may decide to use a lower pitch, while Vashti might inspire you to make your voice a little higher. As you vary your voice, point to the character who is speaking. Changing your facial expressions and body language can work with a change in voice to communicate a different perspective. For example, when Vashti says "Hmmph!" you might scrunch up your face, raise your shoulders, and grunt the word.

Sing Along

Teachers know that the repetition and rhythm in songs help young children internalize new vocabulary. Use the text and illustrations on the pages of The Dot to spark a little song. You might sing "Somewhere Over the Rainbow", "The Rainbow Connection", or "This Little Light of Mine". You might also sing "The Dot Song" and do some of the movements that go along with it. Include any other songs or rhymes that are inspired by the illustrations or text.

Corduroy
written and illustrated by Don Freeman

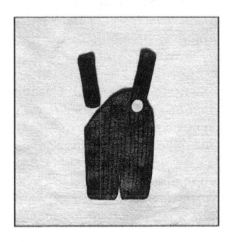

Classic book about a bear living in a department store, hoping for a real home
Features: engaging, narrative text; ink and watercolor illustrations

Recognize Letters and Words

Teachers use repetitive text to introduce young children to letters and words. Small words are powerful tools for emphasizing letter recognition and introducing the concept that individual letters strung together can create familiar words. Every time the word *button* appears in <u>Corduroy</u>, point to it, say it, spell it, and then say it again. You might say:

> *This is the word* button. *The letters* b-u-t-t-o-n *spell* button. *Look, here is the word* button *again.* Button *begins with the letter* B. *Buh, buh,* B. *A capital* B *is a letter made with one straight line and two curved lines. We can find the word* button *on many pages of this book. I am going to point to the word* button *on this page. Buh, buh,* button.

Point to the letters as you say each one and trace each letter with your finger.

Recognize Expressions and Emotions

Illustrators often vary a character's expressions or body language in order to convey a particular emotion. The characters in <u>Corduroy</u> are very expressive. Explain how you can tell what the characters are feeling by looking carefully at the illustrations. For example, on the page where Lisa is leaving the department store with her mother, you might say:

> *I think Lisa and Corduroy are feeling a little sad. I can tell because their faces look sad. Their mouths are turned down and Lisa's eyebrows are going up a little. I think they are sad because they really wanted to be together, but Lisa could not buy Corduroy.*

Later, when Lisa runs up the stairs with Corduroy, you might say:

> *I think Lisa and Corduroy are feeling happy now. I can tell because Lisa has a big smile on her face. Also, it looks like she is running as fast as she can. Sometimes people have a lot of energy when they are excited or happy.*

On the last page, you might say:

> *I think Corduroy is happy that Lisa brought him home. He is smiling and snuggling with her when she hugs him.*

As you read, mimic the expressions of the characters. You might say:

> *This is how I look when I am excited like Lisa* [express excitement].

Predict and Pretend

Teachers often ask children to predict, pretend, ask questions, and think critically while they are reading. These are important tools for comprehension and advanced interaction between the reader and a book. As you read Corduroy, expose your little one to language and interactive thoughts by modeling these tools. For example, after reading the page where the security guard says, "How did *you* get upstairs?", think aloud about why Corduroy is searching so hard for his lost button. You might say:

> *Corduroy has been searching all over the store for his missing button. I think it is important for Corduroy to find his button because he heard Lisa's mother mention that his button was missing. That was one of the reasons they did not buy him. He must really want someone to take him home. It looks like Corduroy climbed under the covers. I wonder if he was looking for his button in the bed or if he was hiding from the night watchman.*

While you predict and pretend, notice how prior knowledge and past experiences influence your conversation.

Make Connections

Educators ask children to make connections to stories and text in order to increase comprehension. Spend some time on each page of Corduroy narrating the pictures. Tell your little one what is happening and make connections. You might link the text to other books, to personal experiences, or to events in the real world. For example, on the page where Corduroy first sees Lisa's room, you might say:

> Look, Corduroy is in Lisa's room. I see a lot of objects in her room that look familiar. She is kneeling down next to a black rocking chair with a pink cushion. I used to have a rocking chair in my home when I was growing up. I loved to sit in the rocking chair and read books. Look at the flower pot on her windowsill. We have flowers in our home, too. Here is Lisa's bed. She sleeps in that bed. You sleep in a crib. One day you will sleep in a bed.

Making connections not only increases understanding, but also serves to honor your child's experiences, and helps your little one view stories through a personal lens.

Consider Differences and Similarities

Teachers know that a basic understanding of comparisons is important for organizing ideas. Use Don Freeman's illustrations to highlight the differences and similarities in Corduroy. First, point out Corduroy and the white rabbit on the first page. You might say:

> Look, Corduroy is right next to the white rabbit. They are both stuffed animals. Corduroy and the white rabbit both have two eyes, a nose, a mouth, ears, paws, and soft fur. They are different, too. The white rabbit is sitting on the shelf, while Corduroy is standing. Corduroy has brown fur and the rabbit has white fur. The rabbit's eyes are pink, and it has whiskers. The white rabbit is also much bigger than Corduroy and is wearing only a blue bow.

Point out any other features that are similar or different. You might even compare all the toys on the shelf. For example, the giraffe has much longer legs than the rabbit, and the rabbit has much longer ears. As you read, point out any other similarities and differences you find in the story.

Identify Physical Features

Teachers often point out familiar features of characters as they read books with young children. With your finger, point out the identifying features of each toy in <u>Corduroy</u>. For example, the bear has fuzzy brown fur and is wearing green overalls. The giraffe has a long neck and brown spots. The bunny has two long ears. The clown has a red nose and striped pants. The turtle is green and has a shell. On the first page, you might say:

> Look at the giraffe on the shelf next to Corduroy. It has a long neck, long eyelashes, and long ears. The spots on its body are brown, and there are two horns on top of its head.

Point out as many features as you can identify in each illustration.

Identify Colors, Patterns, and Shapes

Educators often ask young children to identify objects and patterns based on their colors and shapes. The illustrations in <u>Corduroy</u> are enlivened with bold watercolors. As you share the pictures with your little one, point out various colors, shapes, and patterns. For example, on the first page, you might say:

> Look at Corduroy. He is wearing green overalls. They have a pattern of faint stripes. His fur is brown. The bunny is next to Corduroy. The bunny's fur is white. This bunny is wearing a blue bow. The doll on the shelf is wearing a pink dress with a blue sash.

On the page when Corduroy steps off the escalator, you might say:

> Look at the lamps. Many of the lampshades are drawn as trapezoids. A trapezoid is a shape that has four sides, with one pair of opposite sides that are parallel. Each lampshade is a different color. See the yellow, orange, pink, and purple lampshades? I am going to point to the orange lampshade.

In Lisa's room, point out the green overalls again. Then say:

> Let's see if we can find something else that is green in Lisa's room. Here are green stripes on the wall.

You can also find shapes in her room. As you read, you might say:

> The rug is round; it is a circle. Look, I can use my finger to trace the circle. The end of Corduroy's new bed is a rectangle. I am going to trace the rectangle with your finger. I see a picture frame that is a rectangle, too.

You may decide to follow one object, pattern, or shape throughout the book or point out different features in each illustration.

Practice Number Sense

Books provide a platform for introducing the concept of number sense and exposing children to an early visual understanding of math. Use the pages of <u>Corduroy</u> to play counting games. For example, on the page with tables, chairs, and beds, you might say:

> *There is a lot of furniture on this page. I see couches, chairs, tables, beds, and lamps in this big room. I am going to count the beds: one, two, three, four, five, six, seven, eight, nine. There are nine beds. We have beds in our home, too. There is a pillow on each bed, so that means there are nine bed pillows, too. I wonder how many lamps there are in this picture. I am going to count the lamps: one, two, three, four, five, six, seven, eight, nine, ten, eleven, twelve. There are twelve lamps. There are more lamps in the room than there are beds.*

As you read, count toys, hats on the characters, steps on the escalator, various types of furniture, buttons on the different characters' clothing, or anything else you find in the illustrations.

Vary Your Reading

Reading with emphasis, or changing the inflection and tone of your voice, helps draw children into the text. While reading <u>Corduroy</u>, emphasize passages with question marks and those with exclamation points by adjusting your voice and tone. For example, when you come to words like *mountain, pop, bang, crash, gasped,* and *cried,* use variations in your voice to convey the sounds and actions. Changing your facial expressions and body language can work with a change in voice to communicate a different perspective.

Sing Along

Teachers know that the repetition and rhythm in songs help young children internalize new vocabulary. Use the text and illustrations on the pages of <u>Corduroy</u> to spark a little song. You might sing "Teddy Bears' Picnic", "If You're Happy and You Know It", "There's a Hole in the Bucket", "The Bear Went Over the Mountain", or "The More We Get Together". Include any other songs or rhymes you can think of that are inspired by the illustrations or text.

Goodnight Moon
written by Margaret Wise Brown,
illustrated by Clement Hurd

Classic goodnight story first published in 1947
Features: colorful pictures, contrasted with black-and-white images

Introduce New Vocabulary

Teachers are aware that books often include vocabulary words or
images that may be unfamiliar to children. As a result, books often
expose children to words they might not hear in everyday
conversations. Goodnight Moon was first published in 1947. The
room in the story reflects this time period. Point out some of the
notable items in the room, such as the corded phone, the drying
rack, the two antique clocks, the copy of Goodnight Moon on the
nightstand, the fire irons, the extra wood for the fireplace, the
baby bunny's slippers, and anything else you and your child may
find interesting. After each full-color spread, there is a black-and-
white close-up picture of some of the items in the room. Talk with
your little one about what you see in the black-and-white images.
For example, on the page with the comb, brush, and bowl, you
might say:

> *Look at the bowl with the spoon. This is a bowl full of
> mush. We do not typically call food mush anymore. I
> wonder what the mush is. I think it might be oatmeal,
> cream of wheat, porridge, cornmeal, or grits.*

Making connections to stories is a tool that educators use to
encourage critical thinking. If you come across these words or

items in other books you share, or in another setting, remind your child that you also saw them in <u>Goodnight Moon</u>.

Recognize Letters and Words

Teachers use repetitive text to introduce young children to letters and words. Small words are powerful tools for emphasizing letter recognition and introducing the concept that individual letters strung together can create familiar words. Every time the word *goodnight* appears in <u>Goodnight Moon</u>, point to it, say it, spell it, and then say it again. You might say:

> *This is the word* goodnight. *The letters* g-o-o-d-n-i-g-h-t *spell* goodnight. *Look, here is the word* goodnight *again.* Goodnight *begins with the letter* G. *The letter* G *makes two sounds; in this word, the letter* G *makes a* guh *sound. Guh, guh,* goodnight. *We can find the word* goodnight *on many pages of this book. I am going to point to the word* goodnight *on this page.*

Point to the letters as you say each one and trace each letter with your finger.

Observe Picture Details

The background details in a picture contribute useful information about what is happening in a story. Teachers often ask children to notice details in the illustrations that may not be included in the text. Spend some time narrating the pictures on each page of <u>Goodnight Moon</u>. Tell your little one what you see and what is happening. For example, when you open to the picture of the fireplace on the first page, point out the flames and the logs, the tools in the stand, the log holder, the mantle, the clock, and the other mantle decorations. You might say:

> *The flames of the fire are reaching high inside the fireplace. I wonder if they just added some new wood to the fire. This special basket on the side is where they keep the wood they will add to the fire next. These are the yellow tools they use to tend the fire. They might use the tools to move the logs or scoop the ashes. I wonder why a fire is lit in the bunny's room right now. I think it is because it is cold outside, and this is how the bunny family stays warm. The shelf above the fireplace is called a mantle. You can see a blue clock and two blue decorations on the mantle.*

While you narrate, you can incorporate what you see, predict what you think might happen, ask questions, speak from personal experience, or even make up a story to go with the picture.

Consider Differences and Similarities

Teachers know that a basic understanding of comparisons is important for organizing ideas. Use Clement Hurd's illustrations to highlight differences and similarities in Goodnight Moon. For example, some of the illustrations are full-color, while others are black-and-white. On some pages, the colors are different, but the illustrations are exactly the same. On other pages, the black-and-white pictures are slightly different from the colorful spreads. Point out specific features that make each picture the same and the features in each picture that are different. On the black-and-white page highlighting the quiet old lady, you might say:

> Look at the quiet old lady whispering hush. She is knitting in a rocking chair. Her yarn is in a ball at her feet. I cannot tell what color the ball of yarn is because the picture has been drawn without bright colors. Let's turn the page. There is the quiet old lady again. She looks exactly the same except that I can see more color now. Look at the ball of yarn. It is green. The ball of yarn looks different. It has rolled onto the rug. The kittens are playing with the yarn in this picture.

Next, point out the changes in the room as it becomes darker. For example, when the little bunny first goes to bed it is 7:00 PM; by the end of the book, it is 8:00 PM and considerably darker. You might say:

> Now that we are at the end of the story, I notice that the fire seems brighter in the darker room. Look at the moon, the stars, and the lights in the miniature house; they also seem to be shining brighter.

As you read, point out any other similarities and differences you find in the story.

Consider the Movement of the Earth and the Moon

Teachers often use books to illustrate basic scientific concepts. The illustrations in Goodnight Moon introduce the concept of moonrise. On the first page there is no moon in the window. On the next full-color spread, the moon is visible in the bottom left corner of the window near the rocking chair. As the story continues, a little more of the moon appears. The same way the sun rises in the east and moves across the sky to set in the west — highest above us in the middle of the day and closest to the horizon when it first appears and right before it sets — the moon crosses the sky at night. This happens because Earth is always turning on its axis while revolving around the sun, and the moon revolves around the earth. Point out the continued reveal of the moon in each full-color spread. You might say:

> On the first page, the bunny is in bed and there are stars outside the window. I do not see the moon. Let's see if we can find the moon on the next page with a window. Look, now I can see a tiny bit of the moon peeking through in the left hand corner of the window near the rocking chair. I notice that each time we turn the page, a little bit more of the moon is visible. That is because our planet, Earth, is always slowly turning and the moon revolves — or circles — around Earth. This makes it look like the moon is traveling across the sky. The bunny has a nice view of the moon from the bed. I wonder if the bunny says goodnight to the moon even when it is cloudy outside.

The next time you see the moon in the sky, point it out to your child and mention Goodnight Moon.

Identify Animals

To help build vocabulary and expose your little one to animals and their features, name each animal in the room in Goodnight Moon. As you turn the pages, point to all the animals you see in the illustrations, including animals in the pictures on the wall. Identify each animal, point out any distinguishing features, and make its sound. For example, on the page that says, "Goodnight room", you might say:

> Look at all the animals in the bunny's room. I see a yellow stuffed giraffe here at the top of the bookshelf. Its neck is very long so it can reach delicious leaves high up in the trees. Here is an elephant sitting at the bottom of the bookshelf. It is grey and shorter than the giraffe. The elephant's trunk is long, so it can pick up food to put in its mouth. Look at the two kittens playing with the yarn. They look alike except for their colors. One is dark, and one is light. Kittens make a "meow meow" sound. There is also a

*tiny mouse near the bunny's bed. Let's find the mouse on
some of the other pages, too.*

Continue until you have identified all the animals in the room.

Identify Colors, Patterns, and Shapes

Educators often ask young children to identify objects and patterns
based on their colors and shapes. The illustrations in <u>Goodnight
Moon</u> alternate between color and black-and-white. On the colorful
pages, the illustrator uses bold colors — sometimes solid,
sometimes in stripes — and a few patterns and designs. As you
share the pictures with your little one, point out various colors,
shapes, and patterns. Include the different colors and designs on
objects in the room and also the background colors of the walls and
floor. For example, on the first page, you might say:

> *Look at the balloon. It is a bright red circle. I see lots of red
> objects on this page. The bed, the rug, the bowl, the fire, the
> window frame, and the barns in the picture above the
> fireplace are all red. The blanket is orange. It is a triangle
> with three sides. The books, pictures, and windows are
> rectangles. I can see their four sides. The brown rug is a
> circular shape. There are also white stars in the sky.*

You may decide to follow one object, pattern, or shape throughout
the book or point out different features in each illustration.

Practice Number Sense

Books provide a platform for introducing the concept of number
sense and exposing children to an early visual understanding of
math. Use the pages of <u>Goodnight Moon</u> to play counting games.
For example, on the page that says, "And there were three little
bears sitting on chairs", you might say:

> *Look, there are bears on this page. I am going to count the
> bears: one, two, three. They are sitting on chairs. Let's count
> the chairs, too: one, two, three. There are the same number
> of bears and chairs. Each bear has two ears. I am going to
> count all the ears: one, two, three, four, five, six ears. I can
> also count by twos: two, four, six ears again.*

As your read, be sure to find and count one cow, two kittens, three
bears, four socks and mittens drying, and five windows in the
miniature house. Count anything else you and your little one can
find in the illustrations.

Vary Your Reading

Reading with emphasis, or changing the inflection and tone of your voice, helps draw children into the text. While reading <u>Goodnight Moon</u>, vary your voice each time you read the word *goodnight*. For example, when you read "Goodnight light and the red balloon . . . Goodnight bears . . . Goodnight chairs," use a different pitch and a softer tone when reading *goodnight* and a regular voice when reading the rest. Changing your facial expressions and body language can work with a change in voice to communicate a different perspective.

Sing Along

Teachers know that the repetition and rhythm in songs help young children internalize new vocabulary. Use the text and illustrations on the pages of <u>Goodnight Moon</u> to spark a little song. On the page with the bunny you might sing "Here Comes Peter Cottontail", "Little Peter Rabbit", or "Do Your Ears Hang Low"? When you turn to the page with the bunny snug in bed, sing a little song to help the bunny sleep. You might sing "Rock-a-bye Baby" or "Lullaby and Goodnight". When you look at the cow jumping over the moon, you might sing "Cat's in the Cradle" or recite the rhyme "Hickory Dickory Dock". Include any other songs or rhymes you can think of that are inspired by the illustrations or text.

Baby Cakes
written by Karma Wilson, illustrated by Sam Williams

Sweet, rhyming interaction between babies and their teddy bear
Features: large, soft pictures incorporating many different babies

Introduce Previewing

Teachers often preview books with children to activate their
thinking before a story even begins. Start by looking at the cover of
the book. Point to the title and picture. Talk about what you might
be thinking as you look at the cover. You might say:

> *This story is called <u>Baby Cakes</u>; I wonder what it could be
> about. The word* Baby *tells me there will probably be a
> baby in the story. There is a picture of a baby right here, so
> I think that is another clue that a baby will be in this story.
> There is also a teddy bear in the picture. The bear and the
> baby are both smiling. I wonder if the bear and the baby
> are friends.*

Point out the name of the author and illustrator. You might say:

> *Karma Wilson is the author. She made up the story and
> wrote down the words. Sam Williams is the illustrator. He
> created the pictures to go along with the words.*

Open the book. Before the title page there is a two-page
illustration of a teddy bear with a ball and a baby walking. Wonder
aloud what they might mean for the story.

Recognize Letters and Words

Teachers use repetitive text to introduce young children to letters and words. Small words are powerful tools for emphasizing letter recognition and introducing the concept that individual letters strung together can create familiar words. Every time the word *baby* appears in <u>Baby Cakes</u>, point to it, say it, spell it, and then say it again. You might say:

> *This book is called* <u>Baby Cakes</u>. *This is the word* Baby. *The letters* b-a-b-y *spell* baby. *Look, here is the word* baby *again.* Baby *begins with the letter* B. *Buh, buh,* B. *The lowercase letter* b *has a tall straight line and a small curved line. We can find the word* baby *on many pages of this book. I am going to point to the word* baby *on this page. Buh, buh,* baby.

Point to the letters as you say each one and trace each letter with your finger.

Recognize Rhyming Words

Teachers know that there is a correlation between recognizing rhymes and reading readiness. Every other sentence in <u>Baby Cakes</u> includes a rhyme. After you finish a page or verse that rhymes, repeat the words that rhyme. Then list additional words that rhyme. On the page with the red wagon in the text box, you might read:

> *"Nibble little Baby Cakes on the feet. Oh, my little Baby Cakes tastes so sweet!"*

Then, say:

> *On this page, the words* feet *and* sweet *rhyme. They both have the same* eet *sound at the end. I wonder if I can think of other words that rhyme with* feet *and* sweet. *Meet, neat, treat, and* heat *also rhyme with* feet *and* sweet. *They all have the same* eet *sound at the end, like* feet *and* sweet.

Identify Physical Features

Teachers often point out familiar features of characters as they read books with young children. With your finger, point out and name identifying features of the boy and the teddy bear in <u>Baby Cakes</u>. For example, the bear and the boy have some matching features, such as eyes, ears, rosy cheeks, mouths, and posture. On the page that says, "Tickle little Baby Cakes. Gooch-a-goo!", you might say:

*Look at the baby and the bear. They are both giggling. It
looks like the baby is reaching out to tickle the bear. I see
five fingers on one of the baby's hands. I cannot see the
baby's toes. The bear does not have fingers or toes. Their
eyes are both closed a little because they are laughing. This
is what I look like when I am happy.* [express happiness].
Point out as many features as you can identify in each illustration.

Identify Colors, Patterns, and Shapes
Educators often ask young children to identify objects and patterns
based on their colors and shapes. Sam Williams uses many colors
in his pictures — sometimes solid, sometimes in stripes — and a
few patterns and designs. As you share the pictures in <u>Baby Cakes</u>
with your little one, point out various colors, patterns, and shapes,
including the small picture and the pattern surrounding the text
on each page. For example, open to the two-page spread where the
child is kissing Baby Cakes on the nose. You might say:

*Look at the tiny pictures above and below the words on this
page. I see a bib with red, white, and blue stripes. There is
also a light brown bear. The bear is the same color as the
bear on the other pages and is wearing a cozy, yellow
sweater. I also notice that there is a yellow border around
this page. The border goes all the way around the edge.
There are flowers in the border. The flowers have orange
petals, circular red centers, and green stems and leaves.*

You may decide to follow one object, pattern, or shape throughout
the book or point out different features in each illustration.

Integrate Actions
Teachers often use movement to enhance a book-sharing
experience. Movement can also help active children access books.
While you read <u>Baby Cakes</u>, help your child understand the
correlation between text and actions. First, point to the babies and
their cuddly bears in each illustration. Then, describe what they
are doing. Act out the motions for your little one. For example, on
the page that says, "Yay for little Baby Cakes. Clap, clap, clap!",
you might say:

*The child is sitting with Baby Cakes. They are facing each
other, and they are both smiling. The child is clapping with
Baby Cakes. I can smile and clap my hands, too. This is
how I clap my hands.*

As you read, demonstrate other actions and movements shown in the illustrations.

Vary Your Reading

Reading with emphasis, or changing the inflection and tone of your voice, helps draw children into the text. Young children love songs and chants, and Baby Cakes lends itself well to a rhythmic reading. As you read the text, try to keep a chanting beat. You might even clap, snap, or tap the beat gently as you recite the words. You may also decide to pause at the end of the second line of each rhyme before reading the last word. For example, you might read:

> *"Laugh with little Baby Cakes. Ha, ha, ha! Sing to little Baby Cakes. La, la, . . . [pause] la."*

As your child's speaking vocabulary grows, he will be able to fill in the missing word.

Sing Along

Teachers know that the repetition and rhythm in songs help young children internalize new vocabulary. Use the text and illustrations on the pages of Baby Cakes to spark a little song. You might sing "The Bear Went Over the Mountain", "Fuzzy Wuzzy Was a Bear", "One, Two, I Love You", or "Rock-a-bye Baby". Include any other songs or rhymes you can think of that are inspired by the illustrations or text.

Five Little Monkeys Jumping on the Bed
written and illustrated by Eileen Christelow

Text version of the classic children's counting song
Features: simple, repetitive, rhyming text; soft, colorful, active illustrations

Introduce Previewing

Teachers often preview books with children to activate their thinking before a story even begins. Start by looking at the cover of the book. Point to the title and picture. Talk about what you might be thinking as you look at the cover. You might say:

> *This story is called <u>Five Little Monkeys Jumping on the Bed</u>; I wonder what it could be about. The word* Monkeys *tells me there will probably be monkeys in the story. There is a picture of five monkeys, so I think that is another clue that monkeys will be in this story. The monkeys are on a bed in the picture. The monkeys look like they are jumping on the bed. I wonder if they are allowed to jump on the bed or if they will get into trouble.*

Point out the name of the author and illustrator. You might say:

> *Eileen Christelow is the author. She made up the story and wrote down the words. She is also the illustrator. She created the pictures to go along with the words.*

Recognize Letters and Words

Teachers use repetitive text and songs to introduce young children to letters and words. Small words are powerful tools for emphasizing letter recognition and introducing the concept that individual letters strung together can create familiar words. Every time the word *jumping* appears in <u>Five Little Monkeys Jumping on the Bed</u>, point to it, say it, spell it, and then say it again. You might say:

> *This book is called* <u>Five Little Monkeys Jumping on the Bed</u>. *This is the word* Jumping. *The letters* j-u-m-p-i-n-g *spell* jumping. *Look, here is the word* jumping *again.* Jumping *begins with the letter* J. *Juh, juh,* J. *The letter* J *is made with a long, curved line. We can find the word* jumping *on many pages of this book. I am going to point to the word* jumping *on this page. Juh, juh,* jumping.

Point to the letters as you say each one and trace each letter with your finger.

Predict and Pretend

Teachers often ask children to predict, pretend, ask questions, and think critically while they are reading. These are important tools for comprehension and advanced interaction between the reader and a book. As you read <u>Five Little Monkeys Jumping on the Bed</u>, expose your little one to language and interactive thoughts by modeling these tools. For example, on the page where the five little monkeys fall asleep, you might say:

> *Look, all the monkeys are finally tucked into bed. I wonder why they kept jumping on the bed. They all got hurt when they fell off the bed. Mama had to put bandages on all of their heads. I wonder if they will feel better in the morning. Look at the mama now. She looks relieved that they are all finally asleep and cannot jump on the bed anymore. If those monkeys were my children, I would be relieved, too.*

While you predict and pretend, notice how prior knowledge and past experiences influence your conversation.

Identify Colors, Patterns, and Shapes

Educators often ask young children to identify objects and patterns based on their colors and shapes. The illustrator, Eileen Christelow, incorporates many colors and patterns into the pictures in <u>Five Little Monkeys Jumping on the Bed</u>. As you share the pictures with your little one, point out and say the names of the different colors, shapes, and patterns, including pajamas, bed sheets, and chairs. For example, turn to the page when the five little monkeys first jump on the bed. You might say:

There are a lot of colors and patterns in this picture. I notice there is an orange checkered comforter on the bed. I also notice that each of the monkeys is wearing pajamas with a different design. The first monkey is wearing pajamas with green trees and round orange suns. The second monkey is wearing a green nightgown. The third monkey is wearing pajamas with orange dots and blue circles. The fourth monkey's pajamas have a pattern of red stripes. The fifth monkey's pajamas have purple polka dots.

You may decide to follow one object, pattern, or shape throughout the book or point out different features in each illustration.

Practice Number Sense

Books provide a platform for introducing the concept of number sense and exposing children to an early visual understanding of math. Use the pages of <u>Five Little Monkeys Jumping on the Bed</u> to play counting games. For example, on the first page, you might say:

Look, all five of the monkeys are taking a bath. I notice that some of the monkeys have a scrub brush or a cloth and are washing their bodies. One, two, three monkeys are washing. The other two are playing. In the next picture, all five monkeys are putting on their pajamas. Some of the monkeys have their hands in the air. One, two, three monkeys have their arms up while they are putting on their pajamas. That means that two monkeys have their arms down by their sides because three plus two equals five. Over here they are brushing their teeth. I am going to count the toothbrushes in this picture: one, two, three, four, five. There are five toothbrushes for five monkeys.

As you read, count towels, monkeys, eyes, tears, bandages, noses, feet, tails, pajamas, and pillows. Count anything else you can find in the illustrations.

Integrate Actions

Teachers often use movement to enhance a book-sharing experience. Movement can also help active children access books. While you read <u>Five Little Monkeys Jumping on the Bed</u>, help your child understand the correlation between text and actions. First, point to the monkeys, the mama, and the doctor in the illustrations. Then, describe what they are doing. For example, in different pictures the monkeys are jumping, lying down, kneeling, standing, sitting, peeking over the bed, throwing their hands in the air, and climbing. The mama and the doctor become more frustrated as the story progresses. Act out the motions for your little one (other than jumping on the bed, of course). Following the page showing the monkey in the green nightgown falling off the bed, you might say:

> *I am going to pretend I am on the phone; I am holding it up to my ear. I am the frustrated doctor talking to the mama. Look at my face. It is scrunched up and I am pulling on my hair. Those monkeys need to stop jumping on the bed!*

Use fun hand motions to emphasize the numbers and actions in the story. For example, when you read the number *five*, hold up five fingers. As you read, demonstrate other actions and movements shown in the illustrations.

Teachable Moment

Picture books often include an important message, or a moral, that resonates with young children. Teachers use these stories to reinforce specific behaviors, teach about right and wrong, or introduce a new lesson. After you read Five Little Monkeys Jumping on the Bed, explain to your child that beds are for resting and sleeping. You might say:

> *Even though it might seem like fun, jumping on the bed is dangerous. If you jump on the bed and fall, you might get hurt. Your body is delicate, especially your head and your neck. The doctor becomes more and more upset during the story because the monkeys keep jumping on the bed, even though their brothers and sisters are getting hurt. The doctor wants the monkeys to be safe. So does their mama. It is important that the monkeys listen to their mama when she tells them not to jump on the bed.*

Vary Your Reading

Reading with emphasis, or changing the inflection and tone of your voice, helps draw children into the text. Young children love songs and chants, and Five Little Monkeys Jumping on the Bed lends itself well to a rhythmic reading. You can sing the song if you know it or make up your own if you do not. Either way, try to keep a beat. You might even clap, snap, or tap the beat gently as you recite the words. After a few readings, you may also decide to pause at the end of the second line of each rhyme. For example, you might read:

> *"Five little monkeys jumped on the bed! One fell off and bumped his . . .* [pause] *head."*

As your child's speaking vocabulary grows, she will be able to fill in the missing word.

Sing Along

Teachers know that the repetition and rhythm in songs help young children internalize new vocabulary. Use the text and illustrations on the pages of <u>Five Little Monkeys Jumping on the Bed</u> to spark a little song. You might sing "Five Little Monkeys Jumping on the Bed", "Ten in the Bed (Roll Over)", "Going to the Zoo", or "Pop! Goes the Weasel". Include any other songs or rhymes you can think of that are inspired by the illustrations or text.

How Do Dinosaurs Say Good Night?
written by Jane Yolen, illustrated by Mark Teague

A playful look at childlike dinosaurs right before bedtime
Features: large type; one question or statement on most pages; large,
detailed dinosaur illustrations

Introduce Previewing
Teachers often preview books with children to activate their
thinking before a story even begins. Start by looking at the cover of
the book. Point to the title and picture. Talk about what you might
be thinking as you look at the cover. You might say:

> *This story is called* How Do Dinosaurs Say Good Night?. *I
> wonder what it could be about. The word* Dinosaur *tells me
> there will probably be a dinosaur in the story. There is a
> picture of a dinosaur right here, so I think that is another
> clue that a dinosaur will be in this story. The dinosaur is
> sitting on the bed, and a mommy is at the door. The
> dinosaur and the mommy are both smiling. I wonder if the
> dinosaur is ready for bed.*

Point out the name of the author and the illustrator. You might
say:

> *Jane Yolen is the author. She made up the story and wrote
> down the words. Mark Teague is the illustrator. He created
> the pictures to go along with the words.*

The inside of the cover shows different dinosaurs in bed, along
with their names. Wonder aloud what they might mean for the
story.

Introduce New Vocabulary

Teachers are aware that books often include vocabulary words that are unfamiliar to children. As a result, books often expose children to words they might not hear in everyday conversations. These words can give information, make a text sound more sophisticated or more like everyday speech, or help convey emotion. The scientific name of each dinosaur in How Do Dinosaurs Say Good Night? appears somewhere on the page. Find each dinosaur's name and pronounce it for your child. On the first page, you might say:

> *There are many different kinds of dinosaurs. Look at the end of the dinosaur's bed. It says* Tyrannosaurus Rex. *That means that this dinosaur is a* Tyrannosaurus Rex. *Sometimes people call this dinosaur a T-Rex. I am going to keep reading and see what kind of dinosaur is on the next page.*

After you finish reading the book, point to each of the dinosaurs on the inside of the cover, saying their names. Making connections to stories is a tool that educators use to encourage critical thinking. If you come across these words in other books you share, or in another setting, remind your child that you also saw them in How Do Dinosaurs Say Good Night?.

Recognize Letters and Words

Teachers use repetitive text to introduce young children to letters and words. Small words are powerful tools for emphasizing letter recognition and introducing the concept that individual letters strung together can create familiar words. Every time the word *dinosaur* appears in How Do Dinosaurs Say Good Night?, point to it, say it, spell it, and then say it again. You might say:

> *This book is called* How Do Dinosaurs Say Good Night?. *This is the word* Dinosaur. *The letters* d-i-n-o-s-a-u-r *spell* dinosaur. *Look, here is the word* dinosaur *again.* Dinosaur *begins with the letter* D. *Duh, duh,* D. *The lowercase letter* d *has a tall straight line and one rounded line. We can find the word* dinosaur *on many pages of this book. I am going to point to the word* dinosaur *on this page. Duh, duh,* Dinosaur.

Point to the letters as you say each one and trace each letter with your finger.

Recognize Expressions and Emotions

Illustrators often vary a character's expressions or body language in order to convey a particular emotion. In How Do Dinosaurs Say Good Night? the characters are very expressive. Point out the facial expressions and body language of both the dinosaurs and their parents and tell your child if the characters look sad, angry, defiant, frustrated, hopeful, peaceful, or relaxed. For example, on the page where the dinosaur falls down onto his bedcovers and cries, you might say:

> *Look at the dinosaur's mother. She wants the dinosaur to say goodnight and go to bed. I can tell by the way she is standing with her hands on her hips, her eyebrows scrunched together, and her mouth turned down, that she is frustrated or angry with the dinosaur because he is not going to sleep. Look at the dinosaur. He is very sad. The dinosaur is very tired, but he does not want to go to sleep. I can tell that he is sad because he is lying on top of his bed and crying.*

As you read, mimic the expressions of the characters. You might say:

> *This is how I look when I am sad like the dinosaur* [express sadness], *but this is how I look when I am happy again* [express happiness].

Make Connections

Educators ask children to make connections to stories and text in order to increase comprehension. Spend some time narrating the pictures on each page of How Do Dinosaurs Say Good Night?. Tell your little one what is happening and make connections. You might link the text to other books, to personal experiences, or to events in the real world. For example, each dinosaur is pictured in his room. Point out the objects in the rooms, such as a bed, books, toys, teddy bears, clothes, wall art, windows, or pets. Next point out anything in the dinosaur's room that your child also has. On the page where the Pteranodon is throwing the teddy bear, you might say:

> *Look, the dinosaur has a fuzzy teddy bear. You have a stuffed toy, too. He also has a pair of blue boots next to his dresser. You have shoes, too. The dinosaur's name is* Pteranodon; *I can see it spelled with the blocks. I think the*

dinosaur lined up the blocks. Sometimes I line up things,
too. Look at all the dinosaur's books. You have books, too.
Making connections not only increases understanding, but also
serves to honor your child's experiences, and helps your little one
view stories through a personal lens.

Consider the Concept of Perspective

Teachers often use books to illustrate basic scientific concepts. The
dinosaurs in How Do Dinosaurs Say Good Night? are drawn big,
and yet their beds and all their toys are human size, so the objects
in the rooms seem little by comparison. Point out to your little one
how the large dinosaurs are trying to snuggle down on normal-
sized human beds, or are holding items that look much too small
for them. You may want to present a small toy to your child to
make a comparison between his size and the size of the dinosaurs.
For example, on the page where the dinosaur "swings his neck
from side to side", you might say:

> *Look at the ball in my hand. It is similar to the ball on the*
> *dinosaur's dresser. I am able to hold the ball in my hand,*
> *but it is smaller than the dinosaur's little toe! The dinosaur*
> *is much bigger than we are, so he makes all the toys look*
> *tiny.*

Identify Colors, Patterns, and Shapes

Educators often ask young children to identify objects and patterns
based on their colors and shapes. The details in Mark Teague's
illustrations in How Do Dinosaurs Say Good Night? offer many
opportunities to point out colors, shapes, and patterns to your little
one, including items of clothing, toys in the bedrooms, and sheets
and bedspreads. For example, on the page with the dinosaur
slamming his tail and pouting, you might say:

> *Look at the dinosaur's father. He is wearing a dark blue*
> *sweater and light blue pants. I also notice the sky outside*
> *the dinosaur's window is blue. This dinosaur is dark green*
> *with brown spots. Each spot is a slightly different shape. I*
> *see other shapes in this picture. There is a building outside*
> *the dinosaur's window. The windows on the building are*
> *yellow rectangles. I also see a pattern on the band along the*
> *top of the wallpaper: Brontosaurus, then Tyrannosaurus*
> *Rex, then Triceratops.*

You may decide to follow one object, pattern, or shape throughout the book or point out different features in each illustration.

Practice Number Sense

Books provide a platform for introducing the concept of number sense and exposing children to an early visual understanding of math. Use the pages of How Do Dinosaurs Say Good Night? to play counting games. For example, on the page where the dinosaur "demands a piggyback ride," you might say:

> This is an Ankylosaurus. He has scaly skin and sharp spikes on his head, back, and tail. I am going to count the spikes. There are two spikes on his head and twenty-nine spikes on his back and tail!

As you read, count the number of sharp teeth, long claws, big eyes, and pointy scales on the dinosaurs. You might also count toys, pictures, books, lights, plants, pets, or anything else you can find in the illustrations.

Integrate Actions

Teachers often use movement to enhance a book-sharing experience. Movement can also help active children access books. While you read How Do Dinosaurs Say Good Night?, help your child understand the correlation between text and actions. First, point to the dinosaur in each illustration. Then, describe what the dinosaurs are doing to delay bedtime or to show their parents that they are ready for bed. Act out their motions for your little one. For example, when the text says, "Does a dinosaur roar?", you might say:

> This dinosaur is trying to show he is upset. He does not want to go to bed. Dinosaurs do not use words to communicate; instead, they make sounds and they roar. The dinosaur is roaring loudly, like this: [Go ahead and roar!]

As you read, demonstrate other actions and movements shown in the illustrations.

Vary Your Reading

Reading with emphasis, or changing the inflection and tone of your voice, helps draw children into the text. The text in How Do Dinosaurs Say Good Night? is written in poetic form. Either the middle and ending words of a sentence on one page rhyme, or the end of a sentence on one page rhymes with the end of the sentence on the following page. You may choose to give extra emphasis to the rhyming words as you read. For example, you might say:

> "Does a dinosaur slam his tail and **pout**? Does he throw his teddy bear all **about**?"

There are also many descriptive words in the text. You may choose to change your tone and give extra emphasis as you read each of the dinosaur's actions. For example, you might read:

> "Does he **mope**, does he **moan**, does he **sulk**, does he **sigh**?"

The first half of the book points out all the negative ways the dinosaurs might react to saying goodnight. The second half details the positive ways dinosaurs can say goodnight. You may decide to read the first half of the book with a more forceful tone and change to a more gentle tone for the second half of the book. Changing your facial expressions and body language can work with a change in voice to communicate a different perspective.

Sing Along

Teachers know that the repetition and rhythm in songs help young children internalize new vocabulary. Use the text and illustrations on the pages of How Do Dinosaurs Say Good Night? to spark a little song. You might sing "Rock-a-bye Baby" or "Lullaby and Goodnight". Include any other songs or rhymes you can think of that are inspired by the illustrations or text.

SECTION TWO

Conversation Starters for Children *with* Verbal Language Skills

There are many different levels of language skills. Tailor your conversations to your child's verbal abilities.

If you ask a question, let your little one answer in his or her own time. Remember, it may take a moment for your little one to process a question, study a corresponding illustration, and formulate an answer. If your child can point, pose questions that ask your little one to point. If your child knows the concepts of yes and no and can communicate those to you, pose questions in a yes or no format. Even if you answer for your child, there is a great deal of learning that stems from having a question posed, considered, and answered.

Remember that your child is young and can only draw from limited experience. If your little one shares a thought that does not align with what you were expecting, try to honor his or her thinking. You might decide to use the extra pages at the back of *Bookworm Babies* to record any funny, sweet, interesting, or noteworthy moments you share with your child.

The Rainbow Fish
written and illustrated by Marcus Pfister

A classic fish tale that teaches about friendship and sharing
Features: clear, conversational text; colorful, sparkling pictures

Introduce New Vocabulary

Teachers are aware that books often include vocabulary words that may be unfamiliar to children, because they do not name something you can point to on the page. These words can give information, make a text sound more sophisticated or more like everyday speech, or help convey emotion. After you have read The Rainbow Fish and your child is familiar with the story, you may want to define these words: *pleased, admire, glare, emerged, alone, wise, suddenly, wavered, peculiar, delighted,* and *finally*. One way that educators explain these words is to add familiar words with similar meanings as they read. For example, on the page with the octopus, you might add the words *came out slowly* after you read the word *emerged*. You might say:

> *"Then suddenly two eyes caught him in their glare and the octopus emerged"* — or *came out slowly* — *"from the darkness." Why do you think the author chose the word emerged? I think he chose the word emerged to illustrate that the octopus did not rush out of the cave.*

Making connections to stories is a tool that educators use to encourage critical thinking. If you come across these words in other books you share, or in another setting, remind your child that you also saw them in The Rainbow Fish.

Observe Picture Details

The background details in a picture contribute useful information about what is happening in a story. Teachers often ask children to notice details in the illustrations that may not be included in the text. Spend some time on each page of The Rainbow Fish narrating the pictures. Talk with your little one about what you see and what is happening. Ask your little one to notice bubbles, sea plants, shells, snails, crabs, clams, fish, octopus, or coral. For example, on the page where the Rainbow Fish finds the cave, you might say:

> *Look at the Rainbow Fish. He is swimming above red sea plants, a yellow and green snail, and a little green crab. Can you point to the little green crab? What else do you see in this picture? The Rainbow Fish is heading toward the wise octopus to hear what she has to say. The octopus blends in with her cave because she is purple. What color is the inside of the cave? Yes, purple. Can you see her eyes? Why do you think her eyes are easy to see?*

While you narrate, you and your little one can incorporate what you see, predict what you think might happen, ask questions, speak from personal experience, or even make up a story to go with the picture. Taking turns with your child while you are narrating is one strategy to encourage anticipation and idea sharing. You might start the narration on each page, then give your child a chance to contribute.

Identify Physical Features

Teachers often point out familiar features of characters as they read books with young children. With your finger, point to and name the identifying characteristics of each of the sea creatures in The Rainbow Fish. On the page with the octopus, you might say:

> *Look at the wise octopus. She has eight long arms. Like a real octopus, she has little round suction cups on each arm. She uses her circular suckers to grasp objects. Can you point to her arms? The octopus also has two bright eyes. I do not see a mouth on the octopus.*

Compare the features of any book characters with those of you and your little one. You might say:

> *You and I only have two arms. We do not have suction cups on our arms. We use hands and fingers to grasp our food. The octopus has suction cups because she lives in the sea.*

You and I live on land. We have two bright eyes as well. These are my eyes. They are looking at you. Where are your eyes? Here is your mouth. Here is my mouth. I can use my mouth to smile at you. Can you smile at me? What else do you notice about the wise octopus?

Point out as many features as you and your child can identify in each illustration.

Identify the Colors of the Rainbow

Teachers often use books to illustrate basic scientific concepts. Help your child understand the title of The Rainbow Fish by pointing out the colors of the rainbow found on the Rainbow Fish. A rainbow is formed when sunlight passes through water at a certain angle. The colors of the rainbow are always red, orange, yellow, green, blue, indigo, and violet. With your finger, point to the different colors on the Rainbow Fish. You might say:

The author, Marcus Pfister, says this is a rainbow fish. A real rainbow has seven colors. Let's see if we can find all seven colors on this fish. One of the colors of the rainbow is red. Can you find a red scale on the Rainbow Fish? The next color of the rainbow is orange. He has an orange scale near his tail. Can you find it?

Continue in this way until you identify all seven colors of the rainbow.

Practice Number Sense

Books provide a platform for introducing the concept of number sense and exposing children to an early visual understanding of math. Use the pages of The Rainbow Fish to play counting games. Pointing to the Rainbow Fish on the opening pages, you might say:

Look at the Rainbow Fish. Some of his scales are shimmering. I wonder how many shimmering scales he has. Let's count them together. One, two, three, four, five, six, seven, eight, nine, ten, eleven, twelve shimmering scales. [Pause to let your child provide the next number in the sequence if she is able.] I also see shimmering squiggly marks on his fins and tail. Let's count those, too.

As you read, count how many fish are on a page, how many bubbles you see, how many legs the octopus and the starfish have, or how many leaves are on the green sea plants. On the last page, you can count how many friends the Rainbow Fish has. Count anything else you and your little one can find in the illustrations.

Teachable Moment
Often, picture books include an important message, or a moral, that resonates with young children. Teachers use these stories to reinforce specific behaviors, teach about right and wrong, or introduce a new lesson. Learning to share is a social skill important to developing friendships, and it plays a role in educational success. Reinforce the concept of sharing in The Rainbow Fish by demonstrating how to share with blocks or other easy-to-grasp objects. First, bring a set of blocks or toys to your little one. If you are using blocks, you might say:
> *Look at what I have. These are blocks. Right now, I have all the blocks.*

Dole out the blocks one at a time, alternately giving one to your child and then keeping one for yourself.
> *I am sharing the blocks with you. Here is one for you, and here is one for me.*

Repeat until all the blocks have been split between you. Then, you might say:
> *I shared these blocks with you just like the Rainbow Fish shared his scales with his friends. Now we both have blocks. Now it is your turn. I am giving you all the blocks. Can you give one to me and then keep one for yourself? Now you are sharing the blocks with me.*

Look for authentic opportunities in your everyday life to point out sharing and make the connection to The Rainbow Fish.

Vary Your Reading
Reading with emphasis, or changing the inflection and tone of your voice, helps draw children into the text. While reading The Rainbow Fish, change your voice to represent the different characters. This will help give your child a clear understanding of who is speaking. For example, when Rainbow Fish is speaking, you may decide to use a higher pitch, while the octopus might inspire you to make your voice very deep. As you vary your voice, point to the character who is speaking. You can also ask your child to point to the character as you read. Changing your facial expressions and body language can work with a change in voice to communicate a different perspective.

Sing Along
Teachers know that the repetition and rhythm in songs help young
children internalize new vocabulary. Use the text and illustrations
on the pages of <u>The Rainbow Fish</u> to spark a little song. You might
sing "Somewhere Over the Rainbow", "The Rainbow Connection",
or "Tiny Bubbles". Include any other songs or rhymes you and your
little one can think of that are inspired by the illustrations or text.

If You Give a Mouse a Cookie
written by Laura Joffe Numeroff, illustrated by Felicia Bond

An entertaining look at the progressive consequences of
giving an energetic mouse a cookie
Features: clear, cause-and-effect text; detailed, engaging pictures

Introduce Previewing
Teachers often preview books with children to activate their
thinking before a story even begins. Open If You Give a Mouse a
Cookie and turn it over so that you can see the picture that spans
both the front and back of the book. Point to the title and picture.
Talk about what you might be thinking as you look at the cover.
You might say:

> *This story is called If You Give a Mouse a Cookie. I wonder
> what it could be about. Look at the mouse. He is the main
> character. What is he holding? He looks very happy. What
> else do you see on the cover? Look at these red sneakers.
> They look too big for the mouse. Who do you think wears
> them? Let's read to find out who wears those sneakers.*

Next, point out the name of the author and illustrator. You might
say:

> *Laura Joffe Numeroff is the author. She made up the story
> and wrote down the words. Felicia Bond is the illustrator.
> She created the pictures to go along with the words.*

Introduce Tracking

Black text on a white background provides a simple platform for helping young children learn that books have words that can be read (or tracked) from left to right. With your index finger, point to the words on the page as you read If You Give a Mouse a Cookie. Start at the left and move slowly to the right and then down to the next line. Then, help your child track with her finger as you read. You might say:

> When I read to you, I start on the left. Then, I read each word that comes next. When there are no more words to read on this line, I go down and start again on the next line. While we are reading this page, I am going to help you point to the words as I say each one.

On some pages you and your little one might point to each word as you read, and on other pages sweep your fingers under the text without pausing on any particular word.

Identify Pronouns

Pronouns can be difficult for young children to grasp, even when the antecedent of the pronoun seems very clear to an adult reader. Whenever you read the word *he* or *him* in If You Give a Mouse a Cookie, point to the little mouse or ask your child to point to the mouse. You might also add the words *the mouse* as you read the words *he* or *him*. For example, when the mouse finishes his milk, you might say:

> "When he's finished, he — the mouse — will ask for a napkin."

You can also ask your little one to whom the words *he* or *him* are referring. You might say:

> This page says: "He'll probably ask you to read him a story." Who is asking for a story? Who will read the story?

This serves two purposes. First, it clarifies the words *he* and *him* used throughout the book. Second, it emphasizes the correlation between text and illustrations.

Observe Picture Details

The background details in a picture contribute useful information about what is happening in a story. Teachers often ask children to notice details in the illustrations that may not be included in the text. Spend some time narrating the pictures on each page of If You Give a Mouse a Cookie. Talk with your little one about what you see and what is happening. For example, on the first page the mouse is wearing a green backpack when he first sees the boy. The boy is offering him a cookie. On the second page, the mouse is following the boy into the house and the boy is holding up the rest of the cookies. On the next page, you might say:

> *Look, the mouse's little green backpack is on the counter, and he ate only a few bites of the cookie. He was thirsty, so the boy gave him a glass of milk. Why do you think the mouse and the boy are both looking at the glass in a funny way? Do you think the glass is too big for the mouse?*

With your little one, continue to point out other details in the picture, such as the cookie bag next to the toaster and the items on top of the open refrigerator. As you read on, notice what the boy carries in his back pockets. While you narrate, you and your little one can incorporate what you see, predict what you think might happen, ask questions, speak from personal experience, or even make up a story to go with the picture. Taking turns with your child while you are narrating is one strategy to encourage anticipation and idea sharing. You might start the narration on each page, then give your child a chance to contribute.

Predict and Pretend

Teachers often ask children to predict, pretend, ask questions, and think critically while they are reading. These are important tools for comprehension and advanced interaction between the reader and a book. As you read If You Give a Mouse a Cookie, expose your little one to language and interactive thoughts by modeling these tools. For example, on the first page, the mouse is walking with a backpack and the boy is reading a comic book. The boy stops reading to offer a cookie to the mouse. Ask your little one a few questions inspired by the illustration. You might say:

> *Look at the boy. He is reading a comic book. I wonder what it says. Look at the mouse. Where do you think he is going? Where do you think he was before he walked here? Do you think he was at home? What do you think is in his little green backpack?*

Next, turn the page and ask your child to look closely at the picture. In order to encourage critical thinking, ask:

> *What do you think the boy was doing before he started reading his comic book? I am looking at his baseball bat*

> *and ball. Do you think he might have been playing baseball?*

It is important to note that there is no right answer to these questions. The idea is to help your child learn to think aloud and practice critical thinking. While you predict and pretend, notice how prior knowledge and past experiences influence your conversation.

Consider the Concept of Cause and Effect

Teachers often use books to illustrate basic scientific concepts. Help your child understand the concept of cause and effect in <u>If You Give a Mouse a Cookie</u>. As you read, explain why the mouse keeps asking for something new each time the boy gives him an item. For example, on the two-page spread where the mouse asks for a straw, you might say:

> *Look at the mouse. He is very small. The glass of milk the boy gives to the mouse is too big. If the mouse tried to tip the glass in order to drink the milk, what would happen? Yes, it would **cause** the milk to spill. That is why the mouse asks for a straw. Now that the mouse has a straw, what **effect** will that have? Yes, he will be able to drink the milk. Look, the mouse finished eating the cookie and drinking the milk. His mouth is dirty. This **causes** the mouse to ask for a napkin. What do you think he will do with the napkin? Yes, he will clean his face.*

Identify Colors, Patterns, and Shapes

Educators often ask young children to identify objects and patterns based on their colors and shapes. Felicia Bond's illustrations in <u>If You Give a Mouse a Cookie</u> are vibrant and detailed. As you share the pictures with your little one, point out various colors, shapes, and patterns. For example, in the middle of the story, there is a picture of the mouse beginning to draw with crayons on a blank sheet of paper. On the next page, you can see that he drew a picture of his family. Ask your little one to point to each crayon on the blank piece of paper and name the color. Then, turn the page to the mouse's finished picture and help your little one notice where the crayon was used. You might say:

> *The mouse is starting to draw with this green crayon. Let's turn the page and look at the picture he drew. He used the green crayon to draw these dandelion leaves. Where else did*

he use his green crayon? The mouse used the pink crayon,
too. What did he draw? Yes, he drew noses and the squares
on his father's shirt. The noses in his picture are all made
with triangles.

You may decide to follow one object, pattern, or shape throughout
the book or point out different features in each illustration.

Vary Your Reading

Reading with emphasis, or changing the inflection and tone of your
voice, helps draw children into the text. On some pages of <u>If You
Give a Mouse a Cookie,</u> the author starts a sentence on one page
and finishes it on the next page. To build anticipation, raise your
voice and draw out the last word on the pages where the sentence
is not finished. For example, on the page where the mouse has
finished his picture and the boy is carrying all the cleaning
supplies, you might read:

"Then he'll want to hang his picture on your refrigerator.
*Which means he'll **neeeeeed** . . . [turn the page] . . .*
Scotch tape."

Sing Along

Teachers know that the repetition and rhythm in songs help young
children internalize new vocabulary. Use the text and illustrations
on the pages of <u>If You Give a Mouse a Cookie</u> to spark a little song.
You might sing "Who Stole the Cookies from the Cookie Jar?" or
"Hickory Dickory Dock". Include any other songs or rhymes that
you and your little one can think of that are inspired by the
illustrations or text.

Where Is Maisy?
written and illustrated by Lucy Cousins

A lift-the-flap search for Maisy and her friends
Features: simple, short, repetitive text; bold, colorful, pictures

Introduce Previewing

Teachers often preview books with children to activate their
thinking before a story even begins. Start by looking at the cover of
the book. Point to the title and picture. Talk about what you might
be thinking as you look at the cover. You might say:

> This story is called *Where Is Maisy?*. What do you think it
> could be about? Who do you think Maisy is? There is a
> picture of a mouse right here. She is standing behind a
> bush. What idea does that give you? I think she is hiding.
> This is a lift-the-flap book; do you know what that means?

Point out the name of the author and illustrator. You might say:

> Lucy Cousins is the author. She made up the story and
> wrote down the words. She is also the illustrator. She
> created the pictures to go along with the words.

Introduce Tracking

Black text on a white background provides a simple platform for
helping young children learn that books have words that can be
read (or tracked) from left to right. With your index finger, point to
the words on the page as you read *Where Is Maisy?*. Start at the
left and move slowly to the right and then down to the next line.

Then, help your child track with his finger as you read. You might say:

> When I read to you, I start on the left. Then, I read each word that comes next. When there are no more words to read on this line, I go down and start again on the next line. While we are reading this page, I am going to help you point to the words as I say each one.

On some pages you and your little one might point to each word as you read, and on other pages sweep your fingers under the text without pausing on any particular word.

Recognize Letters and Words

Teachers use repetitive text to introduce young children to letters and words. Small words are powerful tools for emphasizing letter recognition and introducing the concept that individual letters strung together can create familiar words. Every time the word *Maisy* appears in Where Is Maisy?, point to it, say it, spell it, and then say it again. You might say:

> This book is called Where Is Maisy?. This is the word Maisy. The letters M-a-i-s-y spell Maisy. Look, here is the word Maisy again. Maisy begins with the capital letter M. Muh, muh, M. A capital M is a tall letter made with four slanting lines. We can find the word Maisy on each page of this book. Can you point to the word Maisy on this page? Can you help me say the letters in the word Maisy?

Point to the letters as you say each one together and trace each letter with your finger. As you continue reading, pause before reading the word *Maisy* to see if your child can fill in the word. To further illustrate the relationship between words and pictures, ask your child to point to *Maisy* in the illustrations.

Observe Picture Details

The background details in a picture contribute useful information about what is happening in a story. Teachers often ask children to notice details in the illustrations that may not be included in the text. Spend some time narrating the pictures on each page of Where Is Maisy?. Talk with your little one about what you see and what is happening. For example, when you open to the picture of the house, point out the flowers, the shrub outside the door, the mail slot, the door knob, the windows, the number five, the roof, the chimney, the bear in the window, and the bear's bow tie. You might say:

> *The brown bear is inside the house. I can see him through the window behind the green shutters. He is wearing a green shirt and a yellow bow tie. Can you point to the yellow bow tie? Look at the house. It is yellow with a red and orange striped roof. I see two planters — or pots — in front of the house. The orange planter has a green shrub with yellow and red flowers. The other is a brown planter with orange and blue flowers. Who do you think planted those flowers?*

While you narrate, you and your little one can incorporate what you see, predict what you think might happen, ask questions, speak from personal experience, or even make up a story to go with the picture. Taking turns with your child while you are narrating is one strategy to encourage anticipation and idea sharing. You might start the narration on each page, then give your child a chance to contribute.

Make Connections

Educators ask children to make connections to stories and text in order to increase comprehension. Spend some time narrating the pictures on each page of <u>Where Is Maisy?</u>. Tell your little one what is happening and make connections. You might link the text to other books, to personal experiences, or to events in the real world. For example, on the page with the sailboat, you might say:

> *The alligator is in the sailboat. He is floating on the sea with a bird flying above the boat. Can you point to the small, colorful flag at the top of the mast? Other Maisy books have the same alligator. His name is Charley. It looks like he is having a good time on the sailboat. Where do you think Charley is going on his sailboat? Maybe he is going to visit his other alligator friends. Would you like to go on a sailboat sometime? Where would you like to sail? Maybe you can sail a toy boat like Charley when you take a bath.*

Making connections not only increases understanding, but also serves to honor your child's experiences, and helps your little one view stories through a personal lens.

Consider the Concepts of Open and Closed

Teachers often use books to illustrate basic scientific concepts. Lift-the-flap books are favorites of many children. As soon as your little one can manipulate the flaps in Where Is Maisy?, let him open and close the windows, doors, tree leaves, and boat sails as many times as he wishes. If your child is opening and closing the flaps over and over again, resist the urge to turn the page. Let your little one experiment with his new-found dexterity and ability to manipulate objects. As your child opens the flap, narrate what he is doing. For example, on the page with the donkey in the barn, you might say:

> You opened the door. What is behind the barn door? A donkey is behind the door. Open. Close. There is the donkey again. Hi, donkey. There are the donkey's ears. Can you close the door? You closed it. Now we cannot see the donkey anymore.

Ask your little one to talk about what he sees. For example, on the page with the bird in the tree, you might say:

> Open the flap. What do you see behind the flap? Now it is closed. Where are the birds? Yes, behind the flap. Open the flap again and we can see the birds in the tree.

Practice Number Sense

Books provide a platform for introducing the concept of number sense and exposing children to an early visual understanding of math. Use the pages of Where Is Maisy? to play counting games. For example, on the last page, you might say:

> Look at the brown planter next to the blue door. It has a green plant growing inside it. Let's count each of the leaves on the plant together: one, two, three, four, five, six, seven, eight, nine green leaves on the plant. [Pause to let your child provide the next number in the sequence, if he is able.] I also see two flowers on the blue door. Each flower has yellow petals and a red center. Let's count the yellow petals on those flowers together: one, two, three, four, five yellow petals on each of the flowers. That means that there are ten yellow petals all together because five plus five equals ten. You have five fingers on each of your hands. If we add all your fingers together, we will count to ten.

As you read, count whiskers, flowers, stripes, doorknobs, apples, and anything else you and your little one might see in the illustrations.

Vary Your Reading

Reading with emphasis, or changing the inflection and tone of your voice, helps draw children into the text. Repetitive phrases can be used to build anticipation. Almost every page of Where Is Maisy? begins with "Is Maisy in the. . . ." As you read, raise your voice and draw out the last word. Then, pause for a second or two before you state the place where Maisy might be found. For example, on the page with the house you might read:

> *"Is Maisy in theeee . . .* [pause for a moment and point to the house] *house?"*

As your child's speaking vocabulary grows, he will be able to fill in the missing word and even begin to recite "*Is Maisy in the . . .*" as you read.

Sing Along

Teachers know that the repetition and rhythm in songs help young children internalize new vocabulary. Use the text and illustrations on the pages of Where Is Maisy? to spark a little song. You might sing "Where Is Thumbkin?", "Open Them, Shut Them", "Row, Row, Row Your Boat" on the page with the boat, or "Apples and Bananas" on the page with the apple tree. Include any other songs or rhymes you and your little one can think of that are inspired by the illustrations or text.

Chicka Chicka Boom Boom
written by Bill Martin Jr. and John Archambault,
illustrated by Lois Ehlert

A classic chant starring the letters of the alphabet
A shorter version can be found in the board book <u>Chicka Chicka ABC</u>
Features: fun, rhyming text; bright, bold pictures

Recognize Letters and Words

Teachers use repetitive text to introduce young children to letters and words. Small words are powerful tools for emphasizing letter recognition and introducing the concept that individual letters strung together can create familiar words. The first and last two-page spreads of <u>Chicka Chicka Boom Boom</u> showcase all the uppercase and lowercase letters of the alphabet. Use these pages to spell out familiar words to your little one. With your finger, point to specific letters and name each one, including the sound each letter makes. For example, when you point to the letter *T*, you might say:

> *Look, this is the letter* T. *Tuh, tuh,* T.

Then, string the letters together to make a familiar word. You might say:

> *We can use the letter* T *to spell the word* toes. T-o-e-s *are the letters we use to spell* toes. [Point to your little one's toes.] *Let's spell some other words we know.*

Help your child point to the letters that spell out his name, siblings' names, or the words *mommy, daddy, bottle,* or *baby*. Spell any other words you use often in your household. Keep in mind that this exercise is not to focus your child on learning the alphabet according to a timetable, or actually teaching him to read, but rather to provide gentle exposure and awareness.

Recognize Rhyming Words

Teachers know that there is a correlation between recognizing rhymes and reading readiness. Each page in <u>Chicka Chicka Boom Boom</u> includes at least one rhyme. After you finish a page or verse that rhymes, help your child repeat the words that rhyme. Then, list additional words that rhyme. For example, on the first page, you might read:

> "A told B and B told C, 'I'll meet you at the top of the coconut tree.'"

Then, say:

> On this page the letters B and C and the word tree all rhyme. They all have the same eee sound at the end. I wonder if we can think of other words that rhyme with B, C, and tree? How about bee? Does bee end in the eee sound? Can you think of another word that ends in the eee sound?

If your child suggests a word that rhymes but is not a real word, you can still support the process by saying:

> Well done! The word you just made up has the eee sound at the end. It rhymes with B, C, and tree.

Make Connections

Educators ask children to make connections to stories and text in order to increase comprehension. Spend some time on each page of <u>Chicka Chicka Boom Boom</u> narrating the pictures. Tell your little one what is happening and make connections. You might link the text to other books, to personal experiences, or to events in the real world. For example, during the second half of the story, some of the letters have special features. On the page with the "skinned-knee D and stubbed-toe E and patched-up F," you might say:

> Look at the letter F. The letter F has a bandage. Sometimes when you get hurt, we give you a bandage, too. The letter F must have gotten hurt when all the letters fell out of the tree. What color is the bandage? Are your bandages green? When I was little, I sometimes had bandages because I scraped my knees playing outside. Have you ever scraped your knees?

Making connections not only increases understanding, but also serves to honor your child's experiences, and helps your little one view stories through a personal lens.

Consider Differences and Similarities

Teachers know that a basic understanding of comparisons is important for organizing ideas. Use Lois Ehlert's illustrations to highlight differences and similarities in Chicka Chicka Boom Boom. Notice any letters that are changed or singled out in the second half of the book. Some of the letters even have special features. For example, the letter *P* is described as having a black eye and the letter *P* in the illustration is drawn with a dark black circle. Flip back and forth between the letter *P* at the beginning of the story and the letter *P* toward the end of the story. Begin on the page with L, M, N, O, and P coming to the tree. You might say:

> *Look at the letter* P *on this page. It has a tall line connected to a curved line. There is a white circle in its center. The letter* P *is to the right of the tree, next to the letters L, M, N and O.*

Next, turn to the page where P, Q, R, S and T are at the base of the tree. You might say:

> *Now look at the letter* P *on this page. It is still a tall line connected to a curved line, but it looks different. Can you spot a difference? Yes, on this page, the letter* P *has a black eye, so there is a black circle in the middle of the curved line. I notice that the letter* P *is still by the tree, but it is on the left side now. The* P *is also next to different letters. Can you point to the letters next to the* P*?*

Next, turn to the two-page spread at the beginning or at the end of the story. Many of the books you read with your little one will be printed with both uppercase and lowercase letters. Pointing out this difference will help your little one to recognize both forms of the letters. You might say:

> *There are two different ways to write letters — uppercase and lowercase. Uppercase letters are used to begin sentences and names. This is an uppercase* A. *Right next to the uppercase* A *is a lowercase* a. *They are both the letter* A, *but they are written differently. Can you point to the uppercase* A? *Can you point to the lowercase* a? *It is right next to the uppercase* A. *What do you notice that is*

different? Yes, the uppercase A *is tall with straight lines.*
The lowercase a *is smaller with a curved line.*

As you read, point out any other similarities and differences you
and your little one can find in the story.

Consider the Concept of Cause and Effect

Teachers often use books to illustrate basic scientific concepts.
Help your child understand cause and effect by pointing to the tree
in every picture of <u>Chicka Chicka Boom Boom</u>. As more letters
climb up into the tree, it begins to bend. You might say:

Look what is happening to the tree; it is starting to lean.
Why do you think that is happening? Yes, the letters are
climbing onto the branches. They must be heavy; they are
causing *the tree to bend. Let's keep looking at the tree. It is*
bending even further. What do you think will happen as
more letters climb onto the tree? What ***effect*** *will too many*
letters have on the tree? Let's see what happens. Chicka
Chicka Boom Boom! All the letters fell out of the tree. What
do you think ***caused*** *the letters to fall? Yes, the tree was not*
strong enough to hold all the letters.

Identify Physical Features

Teachers often point out familiar features of characters as they
read books with young children. With your finger, point to and
name the identifying characteristics of each of the letters in
<u>Chicka Chicka Boom Boom</u>. In the second half of the book, the
letters receive human characteristics, like skinned-knee D,
stubbed-toe E, and loose-tooth T. Help your child point to
corresponding body parts as you read about knees, toes, eyes, and
teeth. When you find D and E, you might say:

This is skinned-knee D. Let's point to the bandage. Can you
put your hands on your knees? This is stubbed-toe E, whose
toe is a little swollen. Can you point to your toes?

When you find T, you might say:

This is loose-tooth T. Can you point to the tooth hanging
down? Do you have a tooth?

If he is not sure where to find his corresponding features, you can
point to your own knees, or toes, or eyes first, then ask your little
one to find his knees, or toes, or eyes, or teeth. Point out as many
features as you and your child can identify in each illustration.

Identify Colors, Patterns, and Shapes

Educators often ask young children to identify objects and patterns based on their colors and shapes. Lois Ehlert, the illustrator of Chicka Chicka Boom Boom, uses blocks of bright colors in her illustrations. As you share the pictures with your little one, point out various colors, shapes, and patterns found on the trees, coconuts, backgrounds, and borders. For example, on the first page, you might say:

> *These are the letters* A *and* B. *What color are they? What color is the* C? *What colors do you see on the tree? Look at the border on this page. I see two different colors. Can you name the colors? What shape do you see in the border?*

You may decide to follow one object, pattern, or shape throughout the book or point out different features in each illustration.

Vary Your Reading

Reading with emphasis, or changing the inflection and tone of your voice, helps draw children into the text. Young children love songs and chants, and Chicka Chicka Boom Boom lends itself well to a rhythmic reading. Try to keep a chanting beat or help your little one to tap the beat as you recite the words. Ask your child to clap, snap, or tap a foot while you read to help demonstrate the rhythm. After a few readings, you may also decide to pause at the end of the second line of each rhyme. For example, you might read:

> *"A told B, and B told C, 'I'll meet you at the top of the coconut . . . [pause] tree.'"*

As your child's speaking vocabulary grows, he will be able to fill in the missing word.

Sing Along

Teachers know that the repetition and rhythm in songs help young children internalize new vocabulary. Use the end pages of Chicka Chicka Boom Boom to sing the ABC song with your little one. Point to the uppercase and lowercase letters as you sing. Sing the ABC song in as many languages as you know. Include any other songs or rhymes you and your little one can think of that are inspired by the illustrations or text.

BIG Little
written and illustrated by Leslie Patricelli

An exploration into the differences between big and little
Features: simple, short, repetitive text; colorful, cute pictures

Recognize Letters and Words
Teachers use repetitive text to introduce young children to letters
and words. Small words are powerful tools for emphasizing letter
recognition and introducing the concept that individual letters
strung together can create familiar words. Every time the word
BIG appears in <u>BIG Little</u>, point to it, say it, spell it, and then say
it again. You might say:

> *This book is called* <u>BIG Little</u>. *This is the word* BIG. *The
> letters* b-i-g *spell* BIG. *Look, here is the word* BIG *again.*
> BIG *begins with the letter* B. *Buh, buh,* B. *A capital* B *is a
> tall letter with one long line and two rounded lines. We can
> find the word* BIG *on each page of this book. I am going to
> point to the word* BIG *on this page. Buh, buh,* BIG. *Can
> you point to the word* BIG *on this page? Can you help me
> say the letters in the word* BIG?

Point to the letters as you say each one together and trace each
letter with your finger. As you continue reading, pause before
reading the word BIG to see if your child can fill in the word.

Observe Picture Details
The background details in a picture contribute useful information
about what is happening in a story. Teachers often ask children to

notice details in the illustrations that may not be included in the text. Spend some time on each page of <u>BIG Little</u> narrating the pictures. Talk with your little one about what you see and what is happening. For example, on the page with the elephant and the mice, you might say:

> *The little boy is riding the big elephant. He is smiling, and so is the elephant. Do you think they are happy? Look at the elephant's long trunk and big ears. I bet it would be fun to ride an elephant. Would you like to ride an elephant? Look at this picture: the boy is looking through a mouse hole. How many mice does he see? Look at their little ears, their little round noses, and their tails. Mice sometimes make a squeaking sound.*

While you narrate, you and your little one can incorporate what you see, predict what you think might happen, ask questions, speak from personal experience, or even make up a story to go with the picture. Taking turns with your child while you are narrating is one strategy to encourage anticipation and idea sharing. You might start the narration on each page, then give your child a chance to contribute.

Consider the Concepts of Big and Little

Teachers often use books to illustrate basic scientific concepts. Every picture in <u>BIG Little</u> emphasizes the differences between items that are big and those that are little. Though the objects in the pictures are different sizes, they are not as profoundly different as objects can be in real life. For example, the elephant in the picture is only a little bit larger than the mice in the picture, whereas an actual elephant is many times larger than an actual mouse. To further emphasize the concept of big and little, you and your child might use real objects in your home, or in your neighborhood, to illustrate the differences between objects that are big and those that are little. You might start by standing up and showing how big you are next to your little one after you finish reading the page that says, "Grownups are BIG. Babies are little." You might say:

> *Look, I am a grownup; I am big. You are a child; you are little. One day you will be big just like me.*

Find other objects to continue the big and little game. For example, you might show your little one a big round ball and compare it with a little frozen pea or another small round object in your home. You might say:

> *Look at these two objects. One is bigger than the other. Can you point to the one that is bigger?*

Continue to look for comparisons. You might even point to a tree and then to a flower as the book illustrates next time you are on a walk. After giving a few examples, ask your little one to find something big and something little.

Identify Physical Features

Teachers often point out familiar features of characters as they read books with young children. With your finger, point to and name the identifying characteristics of the boy in <u>BIG Little</u>. On the first two-page spread, point out his features, including his tuft of hair, his eyes, nose, mouth, ears, rosy cheeks, diaper, arms, hands, fingers, legs, and toes. To emphasize the theme of the story, be sure to note that the little boy's head is bigger than his toes. You might say:

> *Look at the little boy. His head is much bigger than his little toes. Can you touch your head? Can you touch your toes? Look at my head. Now look at my toes. Is my head bigger than my toes? Do you think your head is bigger than your toes?*

As an extension, put your child's hand up against yours to show that your hand is big, while hers is little. Compare the size of your feet to show that your feet are big, while hers are little. Point out as many features as you and your child can identify in each illustration.

Identify Colors, Patterns, and Shapes

Educators often ask young children to identify objects and patterns based on their colors and shapes. Leslie Patricelli, the author and illustrator of <u>BIG Little</u>, creates bright, bold images. As you share the pictures with your little one, point out various colors, shapes, and patterns, including the lattice pattern on the elephant's blanket, the waves in the lake, and the icing on the cake. For example, on the page comparing ladies with ladybugs, you might say:

> *The lady's shirt is red with round, black polka dots. Are her eyes round, too? Her skirt is a darker red than her shirt. What else do you notice that is red? Yes, her shoes and her*

*lips are red, too. Look, under the lady is a shadow that is
orange. Do you see something else that is orange? What
color is the background on this page?*

You may decide to follow one object, pattern, or shape throughout
the book or point out different features in each illustration.

Practice Number Sense

Books provide a platform for introducing the concept of number
sense and exposing children to an early visual understanding of
math. Use the pages of <u>BIG Little</u> to play counting games. For
example, on the page with the ladybugs, you might say:

*The boy is looking at ladybugs with his magnifying glass.
There is one big ladybug under the glass. Do you see the
spots on the ladybug? Let's count the spots together: one,
two, three.* [Pause to let your child provide the next
number in the sequence if she is able.] *There are a few
smaller ladybugs to the right of the magnifying glass. Let's
count those ladybugs too: one, two, three, four. That means
there are five ladybugs all together because four plus one is
five.*

With your little one, count the number of mice you see, the wheels
on the truck and on the tricycle, the ladybugs, the candles on the
cake, the windows on the boat, the ducks in the bathtub, and the
number of big or little items in the book. Count anything else that
you and your little one can find in the illustrations.

Vary Your Reading

Reading with emphasis, or changing the inflection and tone of your
voice, helps draw children into the text. While you are reading <u>BIG
Little</u>, vary your voice each time you read the words *BIG* and *little*.
For example, you and your little one can lower and extend your
voices in a booming way for the word *BIG*, and use higher, sweeter
voices for the word *little*. Changing your facial expressions and
body language can work with a change in voice to communicate a
different perspective.

Sing Along

Teachers know that the repetition and rhythm in songs help young
children internalize new vocabulary. Use the text and illustrations
on the pages of <u>BIG Little </u>to spark a little song. You might sing
"I'm a Little Teapot", "Head, Shoulders, Knees, and Toes" or

"Hickory Dickory Dock" on the page with the mice, "Row, Row, Row Your Boat" on the page with the boat, or "The Wheels on the Bus" on the page with the bus. Include any other songs or rhymes you and your little one can think of that are inspired by the illustrations or text.

Don't Let the Pigeon Drive the Bus!
written and illustrated by Mo Willems

A pigeon's desperate attempt to get the reader to let him drive a bus
Features: clear, conversational type; Caldecott Honor Book

Recognize Letters and Words

Teachers use repetitive text to introduce young children to letters and words. Small words are powerful tools for emphasizing letter recognition and introducing the concept that individual letters strung together can create familiar words. Every time the word *bus* appears in <u>Don't Let the Pigeon Drive the Bus!</u>, point to it, say it, spell it, and then say it again. You might say:

> *This book is called <u>Don't Let the Pigeon Drive the Bus!</u>. This is the word* bus. *The letters* b-u-s *spell* bus. *Look, here is the word* bus *again.* Bus *begins with the letter* B. *Buh, buh,* B. *The lowercase letter* b *has a tall, straight line and one rounded line. We can find the word* bus *on many pages of this book. I am going to point to the word* bus *on this page. The pigeon wants to drive the* bus. *Buh, buh,* bus. *Can you point to the word* bus *on this page? Can you help me say the letters in the word* bus?

Point to the letters as you say each one together and trace each letter with your finger. As you continue reading, pause before reading the word *bus* to see if your child can fill in the word. To further illustrate the relationship between words and pictures, ask your child to point to the *bus* in the illustrations.

Recognize Conversation

Teachers are aware that understanding the conversational nature of a story is an important reading skill for very young children. The bus driver in <u>Don't Let the Pigeon Drive the Bus!</u> speaks directly to the reader. The pigeon who stars in the story also speaks directly to the reader throughout the book, as if he is having a conversation. Point out the bus driver on the title page as you read his instructions. Then, point to the bus driver's words inside the speech bubble. Explain that the words in the bubble are being spoken by the person to whom the bubble is pointing. You might say:

> *See this shape with a point? It is called a speech bubble. Part of the speech bubble is pointing to the bus driver. That means that he is the one saying the words inside the bubble. He is saying, "Don't let the pigeon drive the bus!" Whenever you see a speech bubble, it means someone is saying something. People in books often take turns speaking, just like we take turns speaking when we are talking to each other. The bus driver and the pigeon are talking to you.*

Point out different speech bubbles in the story and ask your child to tell you who is saying the words. Whenever the pigeon asks to drive the bus, pause to give your child time to answer *No!* before continuing to the pigeon's next response or question.

Observe Picture Details

The background details in a picture contribute useful information about what is happening in a story. Teachers often ask children to notice details in the illustrations that may not be included in the text. Spend some time narrating the pictures on each page of <u>Don't Let the Pigeon Drive the Bus!</u>. Talk with your little one about what you see and what is happening. For example, on the last page, the pigeon turns his attention to a red truck. Find the first image of the large, red truck. You might say:

> *This is the tire of the truck. What do you notice about the edge of the tire? Can you find the truck's light? When do you think the driver turns on the lights? Yes, the driver will turn on the lights when it is dark. This part on the front of the truck is called a bumper. This part under the door is called a side step. When do you think the driver uses the side step? Would you like to ride in a truck?*

Turn the page and compare the same features on the smaller truck. While you narrate, you and your little one can incorporate what you see, predict what you think might happen, ask questions, speak from personal experience, or even make up a story to go with the picture. Taking turns with your child while you are narrating is one strategy to encourage anticipation and idea sharing. You might start the narration on each page, then give your child a chance to contribute. As an extension, point out any trucks you see in real life. Together with your little one, name the parts of the truck that are the same as the details you noticed in Don't Let the Pigeon Drive the Bus!.

Recognize Expressions and Emotions
Illustrators often vary a character's expressions or body language in order to convey a particular emotion. In Don't Let the Pigeon Drive the Bus!, the pigeon's eyes, mouth, and body language are very expressive. Explain to your little one that the reader can tell what the pigeon is feeling by looking carefully at how his eyes and body change in each picture. For example, on the page where the pigeon says, "Pigeon at the wheel!", you might say:

> *The pigeon is imagining himself driving the bus. He looks excited. I can tell that he is excited because his eye is wide open. What do you notice about his wings? Yes, his wings are up in the air with movement lines next to them. He has one leg in the air. What do you think he is doing? Dancing? Jumping?*

As you read, mimic the expressions of the characters. You might say:

> *This is how I look when I am excited like the pigeon* [express excitement]. *Can you show me how you look when you are excited?*

Predict and Pretend
Teachers often ask children to predict, pretend, ask questions, and think critically while they are reading. These are important tools for comprehension and advanced interaction between the reader and a book. As you read Don't Let the Pigeon Drive the Bus!, expose your little one to language and interactive thoughts by modeling these tools. For example, after reading the opening instructions from the bus driver, you might say:

The bus driver has to leave for a little while. Where do you think he is going? Maybe he is going to have lunch. I wonder why he does not want the pigeon to drive the bus.

On the end pages, when the pigeon is dreaming about driving the truck, you might say:

Boy, that pigeon really wanted to drive the bus. He was willing to do just about anything! He must really love buses. Do you think he loves trucks, too? Maybe he likes all big vehicles. Do you think he has actually driven a bus before, or is he only dreaming about it?

It is important to note that there is no right answer to these questions. The idea is to help your child learn to think aloud and practice critical thinking. While you predict and pretend, notice how prior knowledge and past experiences influence your conversation. You might also tell your child about something you dreamed about doing when you were a child.

Identify Physical Features

Teachers often point out familiar features of characters as they read books with young children. With your finger, point to and name the identifying characteristics of the pigeon in all his various moods and positions in Don't Let the Pigeon Drive the Bus!. Looking at the front cover, you might say:

Look at the pigeon. He looks very innocent. Look at his eye. It is wide open and he is looking at you. Where do you think his other eye is? Can you point to the pigeon's wing? He has it folded neatly next to his body. Look at the pigeon's beak. What color is it? These are his two legs. He is standing very still.

Point out as many features as you and your child can identify in each illustration.

Practice Number Sense

Books provide a platform for introducing the concept of number sense and exposing children to an early visual understanding of math. Use the pages of Don't Let the Pigeon Drive the Bus! to play counting games. For example, on the first page, you might say:

How many legs does the pigeon have? Yes, two. He also has two feet. How many toes does he have on each foot? Yes, three. How many toes do you have? Do you and the pigeon have the same number of toes? No? Who has more toes? I notice that he has two wings. He also has two eyes. Where is his other eye?

As you read, help your child count the feathers as the pigeon yells to drive the bus, the number of times you see the pigeon's eye, or the number of words in each speech bubble. On the end pages, count the buses, the trucks, the wheels, the windows, and all the different positions the pigeon is in as he dreams about driving. Count anything else you and your little one can find in the illustrations.

Integrate Actions

Teachers often use movement to enhance a book-sharing experience. Movement can also help active children access books. While you read <u>Don't Let the Pigeon Drive the Bus!</u>, help your child understand the correlation between text and actions. First, ask your little one to point to the pigeon in each illustration. Then, describe what the pigeon is doing. For example, throughout the story the pigeon is sitting, standing, bending over, whispering, running, lying down, having a tantrum, walking, and standing still. Ask your little one to act out these motions. On the page where the pigeon says, "I'll go first!", you might say:

Look, the pigeon is racing to the bus. He wants to be the first one there. Do you think he is running fast? Yes, his wings are pumping, and his legs are off the ground. There are movement lines around his body and a zigzag on the ground beneath him. He must really want to play "Drive the Bus." Can you show me how fast you can run?

As you read, ask your little one to demonstrate other actions and movements shown in the illustrations.

Vary Your Reading

Reading with emphasis, or changing the inflection and tone of your voice, helps draw children into the text. While reading <u>Don't Let the Pigeon Drive the Bus!</u>, emphasize passages with question marks or exclamation points by adjusting your voice and tone. You can also use your voice to highlight the pigeon's emotions. For example, the pigeon is pleading with you by the end of the story. Use variations in your voice to portray the pigeon's urgency as you read aloud. Changing your facial expressions and body language can work with a change in voice to communicate a different perspective.

Sing Along
Teachers know that the repetition and rhythm in songs help young children internalize new vocabulary. Use the text and illustrations on the pages of <u>Don't Let the Pigeon Drive the Bus!</u> to spark a little song. You might sing "The Wheels on the Bus", "Little Red Wagon", or "Down by the Station". Include any other songs or rhymes you and your little one can think of that are inspired by the illustrations or text.

Daddy Kisses
written by Anne Gutman, illustrated by Georg Hallensleben

A loving look at daddy animals kissing their babies
Features: clear, repetitive text; soft, painted illustrations

Introduce Previewing

Teachers often preview books with children to activate their
thinking before a story even begins. Start by looking at the cover of
the book. Point to the title and picture. Talk about what you might
be thinking as you look at the cover. You might say:

> *This story is called* Daddy Kisses. *What do you think it
> could be about? Does the word* Daddy *in the title give you a
> hint? What animal is in the picture?*

Point out the name of the author and illustrator. You might say:

> *Anne Gutman is the author. She made up the story and
> wrote down the words. Georg Hallensleben is the
> illustrator. He created the pictures to go along with the
> words.*

Recognize Letters and Words

Teachers use repetitive text to introduce young children to letters
and words. Small words are powerful tools for emphasizing letter
recognition and introducing the concept that individual letters
strung together can create familiar words. Every time the word
kiss appears in Daddy Kisses, point to it, say it, spell it, and then
say it again. Point to the individual letters as you say each one.
You might say:

This book is called <u>Daddy Kisses</u>. This is the word kiss. *The letters* k-i-s-s *spell* kiss. *Look, here is the word* kiss *again.* Kiss *begins with the letter* K. *Kuh, kuh,* K. *The letter* K *has a long straight line and two smaller straight lines that stick out to the side. We can find the word* kiss *on many pages of this book. Kuh, kuh,* kiss. *Can you point to the word* kiss *on this page? Can you help me say the letters in the word* kiss?

Point to the letters as you say each one together and trace each letter with your finger. As you continue reading, pause before reading the word *kiss* to see if your child can fill in the word.

Consider Differences and Similarities

Teachers know that a basic understanding of comparisons is important for organizing ideas. Use the illustrations to highlight differences and similarities in <u>Daddy Kisses</u>. On each page, help your little one point out the daddy animal and his offspring, and explain a difference and a similarity. For example, on the page with the lions, you might say:

Look, both of the animals on this page are lions. The lions look different, though. The daddy lion has a mane. A mane is the longer fur around a lion's face. Does the baby lion have a mane? When do you think the baby's mane will grow?

On the page with the squirrels, you might say:

Look at the daddy squirrel and his little pup. I notice that the daddy squirrel is bigger than the pup. What features do they have in common? That is right, they both have the same color fur. Yes, they both have black eyes and a long tail.

On the page with the man and the boy, you might say:

Here is a picture of a man and his son. Is the man bigger or smaller than his son? I notice they both have dark hair and similar skin color. Do we have similar hair color? They are both human.

Tell your child that even though she is smaller than her parents now, someday she will be grown up, too. As you read, point out any other similarities and differences that you and your little one can find in the story.

Identify Physical Features

Teachers often point out familiar features of characters as they read books with young children. Each daddy animal in <u>Daddy Kisses</u> gives his little one a kiss on a different body part. With your finger, point to and name each animal's body part in the illustrations. Then, point out the corresponding body part on your child and give her a kiss, too. For example, on the page with the daddy bunny and the baby bunny, you might say:

> *Look at the bunnies. The daddy bunny is kissing his baby bunny on the ear. Can you point to your ear? I am going to give it a gentle kiss, too. What else do you see on the bunnies? Yes, they also have black eyes, pink noses, soft fur, and white cottony tails.*

Point out as many features as you and your child can identify in each illustration.

Identify Animals

To help build vocabulary and expose your little one to animals and their features, name each animal in <u>Daddy Kisses</u>. As you turn the pages, point to each animal, identify it, make its sound, and reinforce the differing names of the adult and the offspring. You might explain:

> *There are often different names for adult and immature – or baby – animals, including humans. I am called an adult and you are called a child.*

On the page with the frogs, you might say:

> *This is a green daddy frog. His baby is called a froglet. The frog and the froglet look alike. Do you see how the frog's legs are bent? Why do you think the frog's legs are bent like that? Yes, it looks like he is ready to jump. They also have padded fingers for gripping and bright yellow eyes. What sound do frogs make? Yes, "ribbit ribbit."*

Identify Colors, Patterns, and Shapes

Educators often ask young children to identify objects and patterns based on their colors and shapes. Georg Hallensleben's illustrations in <u>Daddy Kisses</u> are filled with warm, muted tones, interspersed with bursts of bright colors. As you share the pictures with your little one, point out various colors, shapes, and patterns, including the fur on the animals, the color of their eyes, and the background colors. For example, on the page with the giraffes, you might say:

> Look at the giraffes. They are orange. What color are their spots? Yes, the spots are brown and each of the spots is a different shape. They are standing in a field of grass. What color is the grass? I can see darker green trees behind the giraffes. There are also mountains in the background. The mountains are dark blue. What color is the sky above the mountains?

You may decide to follow one object, pattern, or shape throughout the book or point out different features in each illustration.

Practice Number Sense

Books provide a platform for introducing the concept of number sense and exposing children to an early visual understanding of math. Use the pages of Daddy Kisses to play counting games. For example, on the page with the wolves, you might say:

> Look at the daddy wolf. He has two ears: one, two. The wolf pup also has ears. How many do you see? Yes, two. That means that there are four ears on this page, because two plus two equals four. The daddy wolf has four legs: one, two, three, four. [Pause to let your child provide the next number in the sequence if she is able.] Now, let's count the wolf pup's legs. Why do you think we can see only two of his legs?

Together with your little one, count spots, trees, flowers, fingers, toes, paws, tails, eyes, the words on each page, and anything else you and your child find in the illustrations.

Vary Your Reading

Reading with emphasis, or changing the inflection and tone of your voice, helps draw children into the text. While you are reading Daddy Kisses, change your voice each time you read the body part a daddy is kissing. For example, lower your voice when reading "Daddy squirrel gives his pup a kiss on the . . ." and raise your voice to read "paw." Changing your facial expressions and body language can work with a change in voice to communicate a different perspective.

Sing Along

Teachers know that the repetition and rhythm in songs help young children internalize new vocabulary. Use the text and illustrations on the pages of <u>Daddy Kisses</u> to spark a little song. On the page with the bunny, you might sing "Here Comes Peter Cottontail", "Little Peter Rabbit", or "Do Your Ears Hang Low?". On the page with the frogs, you might sing "Five Little Speckled Frogs". Include any other songs or rhymes you and your little one can think of that are inspired by the illustrations or text.

I Love You Through and Through
written by Bernadette Rossetti-Shustak,
illustrated by Caroline Jayne Church

An up-close and loving look at the personality traits
and body parts of one little boy and his teddy bear
Features: large, simple text; bold, colorful, engaging pictures

Introduce Previewing

Teachers often preview books with children to activate their
thinking before a story even begins. Start by looking at the cover of
the book. Point to the title and picture. Talk about what you might
be thinking as you look at the cover. You might say:

> *This story is called <u>I Love You Through and Through</u>.
> What do you think it could be about? Does the word* Love *in
> the title give you a hint? Who is in the picture? I noticed
> that the boy and the teddy bear are both smiling. I wonder
> if they love each other.*

Point out the name of the author and the illustrator. You might
say:

> *Bernadette Rossetti-Shustak is the author. She made up the
> story and wrote down the words. Caroline Jayne Church is
> the illustrator. She created the pictures to go along with the
> words.*

Introduce Tracking

Black text on a colored background provides a simple platform for
helping young children learn that books have words that can be

read (or tracked) from left to right. With your index finger, point to the words on the page as you read I Love You Through and Through. Start at the left and move slowly to the right and then down to the next line. Then, help your child track with her finger as you read. You might say:

> When I read to you, I start on the left. Then, I read each word that comes next. When there are no more words to read on this line, I go down and start again on the next line. While we are reading this page, I am going to help you point to the words as I say each one.

On some pages you and your little one might point to each word as you read, and on other pages sweep your fingers under the text without pausing on any particular word.

Recognize Letters and Words

Teachers use repetitive text to introduce young children to letters and words. Small words are powerful tools for emphasizing letter recognition and introducing the concept that individual letters strung together can create familiar words. Each time the word *love* appears in I Love You Through and Through, point to it, say it, spell it, and then say it again. You might say:

> This book is called I Love You Through and Through. This is the word Love. The letters l-o-v-e spell love. Look, here is the word love again. Love begins with the letter L. Luh, luh, L. The lowercase letter l is a tall, straight line. We can find the word love on many pages of this book. Luh, luh, love. Can you point to the word love on this page? Can you help me say the letters in the word love?

Point to the letters as you say each one together and trace each letter with your finger. As you continue reading, pause before reading the word *love* to see if your child can fill in the word.

Recognize Expressions and Emotions

Illustrators often vary a character's expressions or body language in order to convey a particular emotion. The characters in I Love You Through and Through are very expressive. In each illustration the teddy bear either mimics the little boy or reacts to one of the boy's many moods or situations. Together with your child point out the *boy* in each picture and talk about what he is doing, what expressions he is making, or how he might be feeling. Then, explain what expression the *teddy bear* is making and what he might be feeling. For example, on the page where the boy is in the high chair, you might say:

> *Look at this picture. What is the little boy doing? Yes, he put the food bowl on his head and his spoon is empty! It looks like he might be crying and yelling at the same time. Now look at his bear. The bear has his hands up by his face. He looks like he is worried. What do you think he would say if he could talk? I think he would say, "Oh, no! My friend is upset."*

As you read, mimic the expressions of the characters. You might say:

> *This is how I look when I am worried like the bear* [express worry], *but this is how I look when I am happy again* [express happiness]. *Can you show me how you look when you are happy?*

Make Connections

Educators ask children to make connections to stories and text in order to increase comprehension. Spend some time on each page of <u>I Love You Through and Through</u> narrating the pictures. Tell your little one what is happening and make connections. You might link the text to other books, to personal experiences, or to events in the real world. For example, on the page where the little boy is taking a bath, you might say:

> *The little boy is taking a bath with his teddy bear. He is raising his arms into the air. Look, I can raise my arms, too. Can you raise your arms? Sometimes we raise our arms when we are happy. I think the boy is happy that he is in the bath with his bubbles and his teddy bear. When I was little I liked to pop bubbles in the bath. What do you like about bath time?*

Making connections not only increases understanding, but also serves to honor your child's experiences, and helps your little one view stories through a personal lens.

Identify Physical Features

Teachers often point out familiar features of characters as they read books with young children. With your finger, point to and name the boy's features and the features of the bear in <u>I Love You Through and Through</u>. For example, on the first page, you might say:

Look, these are the boy's toes. He has one, two, three, four, five toes on each foot. Look at your toes. How many toes do you have? Yes, you have five toes on each foot, too. Look at the bear. He does not have any toes. He has round paws. Both the boy and the bear have two ears. The illustrator drew their ears the same. Where are your ears? They look just like my ears. Their eyes are drawn the same, too. What shape are their eyes? Yes, their eyes are both round dots. I am looking at you with my eyes. I can blink my eyes. Can you blink your eyes?

Point out as many features as you and your child can identify in each illustration.

Identify Colors, Patterns, and Shapes

Educators often ask young children to identify objects and patterns based on their colors and shapes. Caroline Jayne Church, the illustrator of I Love You Through and Through, uses bright, bold colors in her pictures —sometimes solid, sometimes in stripes — and a few patterns, designs, and shapes. As you share the illustrations with your little one, point out and name different colors, designs, shapes, and also the background colors and papers in each illustration. For example, on the first page of the story, you might say:

Look at what the boy is wearing. He is wearing a striped shirt. What color are the stripes? Look at the boy's shorts. What color are his shorts? The boy and the bear both have rosy red cheeks. It looks like they are sitting on a black line. Maybe the line is their shadow. The words on the page are also black. The whole page is colored deep purple. What is your favorite color on this page? Both the bear and the boy have eyes that look like black circles. Do you see any other circles on this page?

You may decide to follow one object, pattern, or shape throughout the book or point out different features in each illustration.

Practice Number Sense

Books provide a platform for introducing the concept of number sense and exposing children to an early visual understanding of math. Use the pages of I Love You Through and Through to play counting games. For example, on the page where the boy cries, you can count his tears. Pointing with your finger, you might say:

Look at the boy. He is very sad. He is crying. I can see tears in the air near his eyes. Let's count his tears. He has one, two, three, four big tears. [Pause to let your child provide the next number in the sequence if she is able.] *He also has one little tear. That means that he has five tears all together, because four plus one equals five.*

Together with your little one, count fingers, toes, ears, rosy cheeks, hands, feet, bubbles, and anything else you and your child can find in the illustrations.

Vary Your Reading

Reading with emphasis, or changing the inflection and tone of your voice, helps draw children into the text. While reading I Love You Through and Through, consider emphasizing words to match what they are trying to convey. For example, when you read "*I love your happy side,*" let your voice go up for the words *happy* or *happy side*. When reading "*and your sad side,*" let your voice drop for the words *sad* or *sad side*. Read each emotion in a way that suggests a specific feeling. Smile when reading a positive word or scowl when reading a negative word. Changing your facial expressions and body language can work with a change in voice to communicate a different perspective.

Sing Along

Teachers know that repetition and rhythm in songs help young children internalize new vocabulary. Use the text and illustrations on the pages of I Love You Through and Through to spark a little song. You might sing "You Are My Sunshine", "Head, Shoulders, Knees and Toes", "You Are the Apple of My Eye", or "The Hokey Pokey". Include any other songs or rhymes you and your little one can think of that are inspired by the illustrations or text.

Brown Bear, Brown Bear, What Do You See?

written by Bill Martin Jr., illustrated by Eric Carle

A question-and-answer classic identifying animals and colors
Features: simple, repetitive text; classic Eric Carle illustrations

Introduce Previewing

Teachers often preview books with children to activate their
thinking before a story even begins. Start by looking at the cover of
the book. Point to the title and picture. Talk about what you might
be thinking as you look at the cover. You might say:

> This story is called <u>Brown Bear, Brown Bear, What Do You
> See?</u>. I wonder what it could be about. The word Bear tells
> me there will probably be a bear in the story. There is a
> picture of a bear right here, so I think that is another clue
> that a bear will be in this story. The bear is walking; where
> do you think he is going? Who or what do you think he will
> see while he is walking?

Point out the name of the author and illustrator. You might say:

> Bill Martin, Jr. is the author. He made up the story and
> wrote down the words. Eric Carle is the illustrator. He
> created the pictures to go along with the words.

Introduce Tracking

Black text on a white background provides a simple platform for
helping young children learn that books have words that can be
read (or tracked) from left to right. With your index finger, point to

the words on the page as you read <u>Brown Bear, Brown Bear, What Do You See?</u>. Start at the left and move slowly to the right and then down to the next line. Then, help your child track with her finger as you read. You might say:

> *When I read to you, I start on the left. Then, I read each word that comes next. When there are no more words to read on this line, I go down and start again on the next line. While we are reading this page, I am going to help you point to the words as I say each one.*

On some pages you and your little one might point to each word as you read, and on other pages sweep your fingers under the text without pausing on any particular word.

Recognize Letters and Words

Teachers use repetitive text to introduce young children to letters and words. Small words are powerful tools for emphasizing letter recognition and introducing the concept that individual letters strung together can create familiar words. Every time the word *see* appears in <u>Brown Bear, Brown Bear, What Do You See?</u>, point to it, say it, spell it, and then say it again. Point to the individual letters as you say each one. You might say:

> *This book is called <u>Brown Bear, Brown Bear, What Do You See?</u>. This is the word* see. *The letters* s-e-e *spell* see. *Look, here is the word* see *again.* See *begins with the letter* S. *Ssss, ssss,* S. *The letter* S *is a curvy line. We can find the word* see *on many pages of this book. Sss, sss,* see. *Can you point to the word* see *on this page? Can you help me say the letters in the word* see?

Point to the letters as you say each one together and trace each letter with your finger. As you continue reading, pause before reading the word *see* to see if your child can fill in the word.

Observe Picture Details

The background details in a picture contribute useful information about what is happening in a story. Teachers often ask children to notice details in the illustrations that may not be included in the text. Spend some time on each page of <u>Brown Bear, Brown Bear, What Do You See?</u> narrating the pictures. Many of the animals in the illustrations are in motion. For example, the bear and duck are walking, the dog is running, the bird is flying, the horse is eating, the sheep, teacher, and children are looking at the reader, and the goldfish is swimming. Talk with your little one about what you see and what is happening. On the page with the white dog, you might say:

> *Look at the white dog. I think the dog is running. I can tell because its front paw is lifted, and its tongue is hanging out of its mouth. When I run, I lift my leg a little higher than when I am walking. Let me see you run. You lift your leg higher, too. Where do you think the white dog is going? The next animal is a black sheep. What do you think the black sheep will be doing?*

While you narrate, you and your little one can incorporate what you see, predict what you think might happen, ask questions, speak from personal experience, or even make up a story to go with the picture. Taking turns with your child while you are narrating is one strategy to encourage anticipation and idea sharing. You might begin the narration on each page and then give your child a chance to contribute.

Identify Physical Features

Teachers often point out familiar features of characters as they read books with young children. With your finger, point out the identifying features of each animal in <u>Brown Bear, Brown Bear, What Do You See?</u>. For example, the duck has an orange beak that is slightly open, brown eyes, a tail, and two webbed feet. Point out as many features as you can identify. On the page with the cat, you might say:

> *Look at the purple cat. What color are its eyes? I notice that its ears are pointy. What else do you notice about the purple cat? Yes, it has long black whiskers, four paws, and a long tail. Look at the purple cat's nose. What shape is it? What color? The purple cat's tongue is pink. What do you notice about the cat's left front paw?*

Point out as many features as you and your child can identify in each illustration.

Identify Colors, Patterns, and Shapes

Educators often ask young children to identify objects and patterns based on their colors and shapes. Eric Carle is a master of using bright, bold colors in his illustrations. As you share the pictures with your little one, point out various colors, shapes, and patterns found in <u>Brown Bear, Brown Bear, What Do You See?</u>. For example, on the page with the red bird, you might say:

> *Look at this bird. What color is its body? Yes, it is red. Look at the wings and the tail. They are red, too. Do you see another color on the bird's wings? The red bird has a black face. It is flying on a white background. What color are the words on the page? Look at the red bird's yellow beak. It is made up of two long triangular shapes. Can you trace the triangles with your finger?*

You may decide to follow one object, pattern, or shape throughout the book or point out different features in each illustration.

Integrate Actions

Teachers often use movement to enhance a book-sharing experience. Movement can also help active children access books. While you read <u>Brown Bear, Brown Bear, What Do You See?</u>, help your child understand the correlation between text and actions. First, ask your child to point to the animals in each illustration. Then, describe what the animals are doing. For example, the bear, the dog, and the duck are walking, the bird is flying, the fish is swimming, the cat is licking her paw, and the sheep and the teacher are looking at you. Ask your little one to act out the motions. On the page with the blue horse, you might say:

> *The blue horse is bending down to the ground. What do you think it is doing? Right, it is finding something to eat. What will the horse use to chew food? Look at my mouth. This is what my mouth looks like when I am chewing. Let me see what your mouth looks like when you are chewing. We do not bend down to eat our food like the horse does. We bring the food up to our mouths. Sometimes we use a fork or a spoon and sometimes we use our hands. Show me what you look like when you eat with your spoon.*

As you read, ask your little one to demonstrate other actions and movements shown in the illustrations.

Vary Your Reading

Reading with emphasis, or changing the inflection and tone of your voice, helps draw children into the text. Use the question-and-answer pattern in <u>Brown Bear, Brown Bear, What Do You See?</u> to vary your voice to represent each animal. For example, you might use your regular voice to ask, *"Brown Bear, Brown Bear, what do you see?*" Next, talk with your little one about what kind of voice a bear might have. Together with your child, use your "bear voice" to say, "*I see a red bird looking at me.*" Changing your facial expressions and body language can work with a change in voice to communicate a different perspective.

Sing Along

Teachers know that the repetition and rhythm in songs help young children internalize new vocabulary. Use the text and illustrations on the pages of <u>Brown Bear, Brown Bear, What Do You See?</u> to spark a little song. When you have the brown bear page open, sing "The Bear Went Over the Mountain". When you have the black sheep page open, sing "Baa, Baa, Black Sheep, Have You Any Wool?". On the page with the green frog, you might sing "Five Little Speckled Frogs". Include any other songs or rhymes you and your little one can think of that are inspired by the illustrations or text.

Click, Clack, Moo: Cows That Type

written by Doreen Cronin, illustrated by Betsy Lewin

An entertaining exchange between Farmer Brown and his
dissatisfied cows, complete with hens and a mediating duck
Features: big, bold type; Caldecott Honor Book

Introduce Previewing

Teachers often preview books with children to activate their
thinking before a story even begins. Open <u>Click, Clack, Moo: Cows
That Type</u> so that you can see the picture that spans both the front
and back of the book. Point to the title and picture. Talk about
what you might be thinking as you look at the cover. You might
say:

> *This story is called <u>Click, Clack, Moo: Cows That Type</u>.
> What do you see in the picture? I see that there are some
> cows, hens, and a duck in the picture. These are farm
> animals. Where do you think this story might take place? I
> see something unusual in the cover picture. It is a machine
> called a typewriter. People used this kind of machine to
> type letters and stories before there were computers. Some
> people still do. You put the paper into the machine, then
> press the buttons — or keys — down, and a letter in the
> machine presses ink onto the paper. I notice that one of the
> cows has his foot in the air over the keys of the typewriter
> while the others watch him type. What kind of note do you
> think a cow would want to type? Do you think the hen and
> the duck are helping the cows in the story?*

Point out the name of the author and illustrator. You might say: *Doreen Cronin is the author. She made up the story and wrote down the words. Betsy Lewin is the illustrator. She created the pictures to go along with the words.*

Introduce New Vocabulary

Teachers are aware that books often include vocabulary words that may be unfamiliar to children because they do not name something you can point to on the page. These words can give information, make a text sound more sophisticated or more like everyday speech, or help convey emotion. After you have read Click, Clack, Moo: Cows That Type and your little one is familiar with the story, you may want to explain these words: *believe, impossible, sincerely, growing, impatient, furious, demand, neutral, ultimatum, emergency, gathered, snoop, exchange, decided,* and *boring.* One way that educators explain these words is to add familiar words with similar meanings as they read. For example, on the page where the cows hold an emergency meeting, you might add the words *secretly listen* after you read the word *snoop.* You might say:

"All the animals gathered around the barn to snoop," — or secretly listen — "but none of them could understand Moo." I think the author chose the word snoop instead of listen to show that the other animals were not supposed to be there.

You can then extend the learning by asking follow-up questions, such as:

Why do you think the animals wanted to snoop — or secretly listen — to the cows?

In addition, you may want to discuss the following (possibly) unfamiliar items as you read: *typewriter, electric blankets, stool, buckets,* and *udders.* Making connections to stories is a tool that educators use to encourage critical thinking. If you come across these words or items in other books you share, or in another setting, remind your child that you also saw them in Click, Clack, Moo: Cows That Type.

Recognize Letters and Words

Teachers use repetitive text to introduce young children to letters and words. Small words are powerful tools for emphasizing letter recognition and introducing the concept that individual letters strung together can create familiar words. Every time the word *moo* appears in <u>Click, Clack, Moo: Cows That Type</u>, point to it, say it, spell it, and then say it again. You might say:

> *This book is called <u>Click, Clack, Moo: Cows That Type</u>.*
> *This is the word* moo. *The letters m-o-o spell* moo. *Look,*
> *here is the word* moo *again.* Moo *begins with the letter* M.
> *Mmm, mmm,* M. *A capital* M *is a letter made with four*
> *slanting lines. We can find the word* moo *on many pages of*
> *this book. Mmm, mmm,* moo. *Can you point to the word*
> moo *on this page? Can you help me say the letters in the*
> *word* moo?

Point to the letters as you say each one together and trace each letter with your finger. As you continue reading, pause before reading the word *moo* to see if your child can fill in the word.

Observe Picture Details

The background details in a picture contribute useful information about what is happening in a story. Teachers often ask children to notice details in the illustrations that may not be included in the text. Spend some time on each page of <u>Click, Clack, Moo: Cows That Type</u> narrating the pictures. Talk with your little one about what you see and what is happening. You might focus on the barn, the farmer, the birds, the cows, the hens, the typewriters, the trees, and the ducks, or pause to focus on one image in any given illustration. Then, spend a few moments pointing out any defining characteristics. For example, on the page where Farmer Brown cries, "No milk today!", you might say:

> *Look at the cows. They are all gathered around the*
> *typewriter. Can you point to one of their black spots? What*
> *else do you notice about the cows? Do you see their hoofed*
> *feet? Pink noses? Ears? Horns? Eyes? These are dairy cows.*
> *I can tell because I can see that the cows have pink udders.*
> *The udders are where the cows store their milk. Can you*
> *point to the pink udders? When do you think the farmer*
> *will milk the cows?*

While you narrate, you and your little one can incorporate what you see, predict what you think might happen, ask questions, speak from personal experience, or even make up a story to go with the picture. Taking turns with your child while you are narrating is one strategy to encourage anticipation and idea sharing. You might start the narration on each page, then give your child a chance to contribute.

Recognize Expressions and Emotions

Illustrators often vary a character's expressions or body language in order to convey a particular emotion. The characters in <u>Click, Clack, Moo: Cows That Type</u> are very expressive. Point out the animals and the farmer in each picture and discuss with your little one what they are doing, what expressions they are making, or how they might be feeling. On the first page, you might say:

> *Look at the farmer. The farmer looks angry on this page. His eyebrows are slanted, and his mouth is turned down. Do you think he can hear the cows typing? Farmer Brown's cows usually do not type, so he is probably confused.*

As you read, mimic the expressions of the characters. You might say:

> *This is how I look when I am angry like the farmer* [express anger], *but this is how I look when I am happy again* [express happiness]. *Can you show me how you look when you are angry? Can you show me how you look when you are happy?*

Consider the Concept of Cause and Effect

Teachers often use books to illustrate basic scientific concepts. Help your child understand the concept of cause and effect in <u>Click, Clack, Moo: Cows That Type</u> by explaining why the animals are making demands. For example, on the page where Farmer Brown first sees the note from the cows, you might say:

> *Look at the note from the cows. It says, "The barn is very cold at night." The cold barn* **causes** *the cows to be cold at night when they are trying to sleep. The cows are asking for blankets to keep them warm.*

Look at the page with the note about the hens. You might say:

> *The hens are cold in the barn, too. This* **causes** *the hens to ask for blankets. Would you want a blanket if you lived in the barn?*

Turn to the page with the cows and hens sleeping in the barn with their electric blankets. You might say:

> *What* **effect** *did the electric blankets have on the cows and hens? Yes, they are sleeping peacefully now. They are nice and warm in the barn.*

Finally, look at the pages with the ducks. You might say:

> *The ducks are bored in the pond. This* **causes** *the ducks to ask for a diving board. Do you think a diving board would*

*make the pond more fun? Look, here is the duck on the last page. The duck is diving into the water. The dive **caused** a big splash. It took Farmer Brown a long time to give the electric blankets to the cows and hens; what do you think **caused** him to give the ducks the diving board right away?*

Consider the Concept of Light and Shadow

Teachers often use books to illustrate basic scientific concepts. The illustrations in <u>Click, Clack, Moo: Cows That Type</u> include shadows made with watercolors. Explain to your little one that a shadow is formed when an object blocks light. When the light cannot pass through an object, a shadow appears where the light does not reach. Shadows are sometimes long and sometimes short, depending on the position of the light. For example, on the page where Farmer Brown first sees the note from the cows, point out the shadow of his hat and face. You might say:

> *Look at this. The sun is shining behind Farmer Brown. His hat is bright yellow from the sun. The sun is casting a shadow on the note and on the wall. This is Farmer Brown's shadow. It is the same shape as Farmer Brown's hat and face. Can you point to the part that is his hat? Can you point to his nose? Do you see where Farmer Brown's beard is? There is also a shadow of the nail that is holding up the note. Can you point to the shadow of the nail? The shadows cover some of the words, but we can still read what the note says.*

On the next page, point out that although you cannot see Farmer Brown standing in the picture, you can tell by the shadow that he is still there. You might say:

> *Farmer Brown was standing here reading the note and we saw his shadow. This is his shadow again. We can tell what he is doing with his body by what his shadow is doing. What can you see in the shadow? Can you point to his arm and hand? Can you tell where his legs are? How do you think Farmer Brown feels about the note?*

Ask your child to point out other illustrations that have shadows.

Identify Animals

To help build vocabulary and expose your little one to animals and their features, name each animal in <u>Click, Clack, Moo: Cows That Type</u>. As you turn the pages, identify each animal, point out any distinguishing features, make the animal's sound, and tell your little one what the animal provides for the farmer. For example, on the page where one hen is holding the closed sign, you might say:

> *Look at these birds. They are called hens. Do you know what sound hens make? Yes, "bok, bok, bok." This flock of hens lives on the farm with Farmer Brown and the cows. Do you know what hens do? Yes, they lay eggs. Farmer Brown takes the eggs from the hens. I think he keeps some eggs and sells some eggs. People can probably buy Farmer Brown's eggs. Do you think the eggs we have in our home came from hens? I can see that each of the hens has a sharp beak. Can you point to their beaks? Hens have pointed beaks so that they can peck food from the ground. The food Farmer Brown feeds the hens gives them the nutrition they need to lay their eggs.*

Vary Your Reading

Reading with emphasis, or changing the inflection and tone of your voice, helps draw children into the text. Sometimes text lends itself to a special rhythm or provides an opportunity to emphasize certain phrases. For example, some lines in <u>Click, Clack, Moo: Cows That Type</u> have similar length and can be read with the same cadence: *"Cows that **type!** Hens on **strike!**"* You can also read lines that are repeated throughout the book with the same emphasis each time. For example, lower and extend your voice for the word *moo* each time it is written: *"Click, clack, mooooo. Clickety, clack, mooooo."* Ask your child to say *mooooo* with you as you read. Changing your facial expressions and body language can work with a change in voice to communicate a different perspective.

Sing Along

Teachers know that the repetition and rhythm in songs help young children internalize new vocabulary. Use the text and illustrations on the pages of <u>Click, Clack, Moo: Cows That Type</u> to spark a little song. When you see the farmer, sing "The Farmer in the Dell" or "Old MacDonald Had a Farm". Include any other songs or rhymes you and your little one can think of that are inspired by the illustrations or text.

Moo, Baa, La La La!
written and illustrated by Sandra Boynton

A fun look at well-known animals and their sounds
Features: classic, Sandra Boynton rhyming text;
whimsical animals on solid backgrounds

Recognize Letters and Words

Teachers use repetitive text to introduce young children to letters
and words. Small words are powerful tools for emphasizing letter
recognition and introducing the concept that individual letters
strung together can create familiar words. Every time the word *La*
appears in Moo, Baa, La La La!, point to it, say it, spell it, and
then say it again. You might say:

> *This book is called* <u>Moo, Baa, La, La, La!</u>. *This is the word*
> La. *The letters* L-a *spell* La. *Look, here is the word* La
> *again.* La *begins with the letter* L. *Luh, luh,* L. *A capital* L
> *is a tall letter made with two lines. We can find the word*
> La *on many pages of this book. Luh, Luh,* La. *Can you*
> *point to the word* La *on this page? Can you help me say the*
> *letters in the word* La?

Point to the letters as you say each one together and trace each
letter with your finger. As you continue reading, pause before
reading the word *La* to see if your child can fill in the word.

Consider Differences and Similarities

Teachers know that a basic understanding of comparisons is
important for organizing ideas. Use Sandra Boynton's illustrations

to highlight differences and similarities in <u>Moo, Baa, La La La!</u>. There are two pages of pigs in <u>Moo, Baa, La La La!</u>. On one page, the pigs are dancing, and on the other, they are simply saying *oink*. Turn to the page with the dancing pigs. Point to the shirts, bow ties, jackets, belts, pants, and canes as they sing "*la la la.*" Next, turn to the following page and compare the two sets of pigs. You might say:

> *Look at these dancing pigs. They are wearing striped pants and holding canes. What else are they wearing? These pigs are singing "la la la!" They are standing on two legs. Now look on the next page. These are pigs, too. What do you notice that is similar between these pigs and the other pigs? Yes, they have the same nose, the same ears, and the same hooves. They are also different. These pigs are not dancing. Are these pigs wearing clothes?*

As you read, point out any other similarities and differences that you and your little one can find in the story.

Consider the Concepts of Open and Closed

Teachers often use books to illustrate basic scientific concepts. The illustrations in <u>Moo, Baa, La La La!</u> introduce the concepts of open and closed. Starting with the front cover, point to the sheep and the pigs. Tell your child that the pigs and the sheep have their eyes wide open, but their mouths are closed. You might say:

> *Look at the sheep. Its eyes are wide open. Look at the sheep's mouth. Its mouth is closed. Look at the pigs. They have their eyes wide open, too. Are their mouths open or closed? Look at the cow. Are the cow's eyes open or closed? Can we see the cow's mouth?*

Next, open the book and help your little one point to each animal's open mouth in the illustrations. Tell your child that the animals have their mouths open on these pages because they are speaking. For example, on the first page, you might say:

> *Look at the cow on the first page. Are its eyes open? What about its mouth: is it open or closed? Yes, its mouth is open because it is saying moooooo.*

Turn to the last page of the book. All the animals have their eyes open, but they have closed mouths once again. You might say:

> *All the animals have their mouths closed now. They are waiting quietly. They want you to open your mouth and*

*make a sound. Can you open your mouth? Can you make a
sound for the animals to hear?*

Identify Physical Features

Teachers often point out familiar features of characters as they
read books with young children. The animals in <u>Moo, Baa, La La
La!</u> are drawn with prominent details and features. With your
finger, point out and name the different characteristics of each
animal, including hooves, webbed feet, paws, udders, ears, eyes,
mouths, horns, tails, noses, whiskers, manes, and beaks. For
example, on the page with the rhinoceroses and the little dogs, you
might say:

> *Look at the two large, grey animals on this page. They are
> called rhinoceroses. Sometimes we call them rhinos. Rhinos
> have very large feet. What else do you notice about the
> rhinoceroses? Yes, they have pointy ears, round bodies, and
> little tails. Can you point to the horns on their noses? Their
> mouths are snorting and snuffing. Look at their eyes. Do
> they look happy or angry? The rhinos look like they are
> angry at the little dogs. What do you notice about the dogs?*

Point out as many features as you and your child can identify in
each illustration.

Identify Colors, Patterns, and Shapes

Educators often ask young children to identify objects and patterns
based on their colors and shapes. Sandra Boynton uses blocks of
color in her illustrations. In fact, each page of <u>Moo, Baa, La La La!</u>
has a different background color. As you share the pictures with
your little one, point out various colors, shapes, and patterns. For
example, on the first page of the book, you might say:

> *What color is this page? Yes, it is green. I can see a white
> cow with black spots. Each of the spots is a different shape.
> This is the cow's udder. This is where the cow stores its
> milk. What color is the udder? What color is the cow's nose?
> What color is the cow's eyelid? Yes, it is grey and shaped
> almost like a half circle. These are the words on the page.
> What color are the words?*

You may decide to follow one object, pattern, or shape throughout
the book, or point out different features in each illustration.

Practice Number Sense

Books provide a platform for introducing the concept of number sense and exposing children to an early visual understanding of math. Use the pages of Moo, Baa, La La La! to play counting games. For example, on the front cover, you might say:

> How many windows are on the cover of this book? Yes, there are one, two, three windows. How many cows do you see? How many sheep do you see? How many pigs do you see? That means there are one, two, three, four, five animals on the cover. Let's count their eyes: one, two, three, four, five, six, seven, eight, nine, ten eyes. [Pause to let your child provide the next number in the sequence if she is able.] I can also count by twos: two, four, six, eight, ten eyes again.

Together with your little one, count spots on the cow, bow ties on the pigs, rhinoceroses' horns, dog collars, cats, any of the animals on the last page, or anything else you and your child find in the illustrations.

Vary Your Reading

Reading with emphasis, or changing the inflection and tone of your voice, helps draw children into the text. Use the shape and size of the animals and words in Moo, Baa, La La La! to determine how much volume and emphasis to put into each animal sound. For example, you might read large animal sounds that are in bold lettering, such as *BOW WOW WOW* with loud, dramatic emphasis, and small animal sounds written in a smaller, thinner font, such as *ruff ruff ruff,* with a quieter voice. You can also repeat sounds over and over to emphasize each animal's sound. Instead of one *baa*, you might say:

> A sheep makes the sound "baa, baa, baa, baa, baa." Can you make the "baa, baa, baa" sound?

In addition, you can make each page more playful by adding other sound details. For example, after reading *"Rhinoceroses snort and snuff,"* ask your little one to actually snort and snuff. Changing your facial expressions and body language can work with a change in voice to communicate a different perspective.

Sing Along

Teachers know that the repetition and rhythm in songs help young children internalize new vocabulary. Use the text and illustrations in Moo, Baa, La La La! to spark a little song. When you have the sheep page open, sing "Baa Baa Black Sheep" or "Old MacDonald Had a Farm". The dogs can lead to "How Much Is That Doggie in the Window" or "BINGO". Include any other songs or rhymes you and your little one can think of that are inspired by the illustrations or text.

Counting Kisses
written and illustrated by Karen Katz

A loving family helps their tired baby to bed with sweet kisses
Features: descending numbers; simple adjectives; colorful, patterned pictures

Introduce Tracking

Large text on a solid background provides a simple platform for helping young children learn that books have words that can be read (or tracked) from left to right. With your index finger, point to the words on the page as you read <u>Counting Kisses</u>. Start at the left and move slowly to the right and then down to the next line. Then, help your child track with her finger as you read. You might say:

> *When I read to you, I start on the left. Then, I read each word that comes next. When there are no more words to read on this line, I go down and start again on the next line. While we are reading this page, I am going to help you point to the words as I say each one.*

On some pages you and your little one might point to each word as you read, and on other pages sweep your finger under the text without pausing on any particular word.

Identify Descriptive Words (Adjectives)

Teachers know the importance of exposing young children to descriptive words that add details to a sentence. In <u>Counting Kisses</u>, each kiss is preceded by an adjective. Point out the adjectives on each page and mimic the kinds of descriptive kisses the baby is receiving. For example, on the page with the number ten, you might say:

> *Look at this page. The mommy is giving her baby **ten little** kisses on her **teeny tiny** toes. I am going to give you **little** kisses on your **teeny tiny** toes, too.*

On the page with the number seven, you might say:

> *The grandmother is giving the baby **seven loud** kisses on a **pretty** belly button. I am going to give you a **loud** kiss too.*

On the page with the number five, you might say:

> *The baby's big sister is giving the baby **five quick** kisses on her **itty bitty** nose. Can you give me a **quick** kiss?*

Recognize Expressions and Emotions

Illustrators often vary a character's expressions or body language in order to convey a particular emotion. The baby in <u>Counting Kisses</u> is very expressive. Explain how you can tell what the baby is feeling by looking carefully at the illustrations. For example, on the first page of the book, you might say:

> *Look at the tired baby. Does she look happy or sad? Yes, she is sad. She is crying, and her eyes are closed. Why do you think she is resting her head on her mommy's shoulder? I think the baby needs to take a nap.*

As you read, mimic the expressions of the characters. You might say:

> *This is how I look when I am sad like the baby* [express sadness], *but this is how I look when I am happy again* [express happiness]. *Can you show me how you look when you are sad? Can you show me how you look when you are happy?*

Identify Physical Features

Teachers often point out familiar features of characters as they read books with young children. With your finger, point to and name the body parts highlighted in <u>Counting Kisses</u>. Compare the character features with those of you and your little one. For example, on the page with ten little kisses, you might say:

> *Look at the mommy in this picture. She is holding her baby's feet in her hands. Where are your hands? The mommy is using her lips to kiss the baby's teeny tiny toes. Look, these are your lips. The mommy has her eyes closed. Look at me. I am closing my eyes just like the mommy in*

the story. Can you close your eyes, too? These are your teeny tiny toes. Your toes are on your feet. The baby in the story has ten teeny tiny toes, five on each foot. Let's count your toes, too.

Point out as many features as you and your child can identify in each illustration.

Identify Colors, Patterns, and Shapes

Educators often ask young children to identify objects and patterns based on their colors and shapes. Karen Katz uses colorful details in her illustrations. As you share the pictures in <u>Counting Kisses</u> with your little one, point out the colors, shapes, and patterns in the curtains, rugs, shirts, wallpaper, tablecloths, couches, chairs, and bedspreads. For example, on the last page, where the baby is sleeping, you might say:

The baby's shirt is pink with red hearts. Can you point to the red hearts? The blanket she is sleeping under is red with white and blue flowers. The blanket also has orange and white square blocks at the top. Can you point to the orange part of the blanket? What color is the sheet in her crib? Yes, it is blue with white, round polka dots. The bumper is green with a pattern of white triangles.

You may decide to follow one object, pattern, or shape throughout the book or point out different features in each illustration.

Practice Number Sense

Books provide a platform for introducing the concept of number sense and exposing children to an early visual understanding of math. Each page in <u>Counting Kisses</u> has a number spelled out, the number itself, and a corresponding number of hearts. Point out these three ways of representing the numbers. First, point out the number, then count the hearts with your child, and then read the word. For example, on the page that says, "seven loud kisses on a pretty belly button," you might say:

Look, this is the number 7. It is written in pink. Let's count the red hearts at the top of the page: one, two, three, four, five, six, seven hearts. [Pause to let your child provide the next number in the sequence if she is able.] *Look at these letters: s-e-v-e-n. The letters s-e-v-e-n spell the number seven. Can you point to the word seven? The number seven is represented in three different ways on this page.*

Help your child find the number, count the hearts, and point to the word for each of the other numbers in the story.

Vary Your Reading

Reading with emphasis, or changing the inflection and tone of your voice, helps draw children into the text. While reading <u>Counting Kisses</u>, change your voice for the different characters and for the type of kisses the baby is receiving. For example, when the mommy gives "ten little kisses on teeny tiny toes," you may decide to use a higher pitch. "Eight squishy kisses on chubby, yummy knees" might inspire you to make your voice deeper. Changing your facial expressions and body language can work with a change in voice to communicate a different perspective.

Sing Along

Teachers know that the repetition and rhythm in songs help young children internalize new vocabulary. Use the text and illustrations on the pages of <u>Counting Kisses</u> to spark a little song. When you turn to the page with the baby snug in bed, you might sing "Rock-a-bye Baby" or "Lullaby and Goodnight". Include any other songs or rhymes you and your little one can think of that are inspired by the illustrations or text.

Guess How Much I Love You
written by Sam McBratney, illustrated by Anita Jeram

A tender story about the immeasurable love between a parent and a child
Features: simple, conversational text; soft watercolors

Introduce Previewing
Teachers often preview books with children to activate their thinking before a story even begins. Start by looking at the cover of the book. Point to the title and picture. Talk about what you might be thinking as you look at the cover. You might say:

> *This story is called Guess How Much I Love You. What do you think it could be about? Does the word Love in the title give you a hint? There are two hares in the picture. Do you think they love each other? I wonder what the hares will do in the story.*

Point out the name of the author and illustrator. You might say:

> *Sam McBratney is the author. He made up the story and wrote down the words. Anita Jeram is the illustrator. She created the pictures to go along with the words.*

Recognize Letters and Words
Teachers use repetitive text to introduce young children to letters and words. Small words are powerful tools for emphasizing letter recognition and introducing the concept that individual letters strung together can create familiar words. Every time the word *Love* appears in Guess How Much I Love You, point to it, say it, spell it, and then say it again. You might say:

This book is called Guess How Much I Love You. *This is the word* love. *The letters* l-o-v-e *spell* love. *Look, here is the word* love *again.* Love *begins with the letter L. Luh, luh, L. The lowercase letter l is a tall straight line. We can find the word* love *on many pages of this book. Luh, luh,* love. *Can you point to the word* love *on this page? Can you help me say the letters in the word* love?

Point to the letters as you say each one together and trace each letter with your finger. As you continue reading, pause before reading the word *love* to see if your child can fill in the word.

Observe Picture Details

The background details in a picture contribute useful information about what is happening in a story. Teachers often ask children to notice details in the illustrations that may not be included in the text. Spend some time on each page of Guess How Much I Love You narrating the pictures. Talk with your little one about what you see and what is happening. Point out and name the environmental details of each illustration, such as the trees, leaves, grass, fences, stones, wildflowers, mushrooms, shrubs, butterflies, insects, meadows, blue skies, and moonlight. On the page with the tree stump, you might say:

Look at this picture. Little Nutbrown Hare is playing on the tree stump. A tree stump is what is left of a tree after it has been cut down. Who do you think cut down that tree? Big Nutbrown Hare is standing on the soft, green grass. There are mushrooms next to the tree stump and little plants growing, too. Can you point to the mushrooms and the little plants? There is a stone wall behind Big Nutbrown Hare. What can you see behind the stone wall?

While you narrate, you and your little one can incorporate what you see, predict what you think might happen, ask questions, speak from personal experience, or even make up a story to go with the picture. Taking turns with your child while you are narrating is one strategy to encourage anticipation and idea sharing. You might start the narration on each page, then give your child a chance to contribute.

Make Connections

Educators ask children to make connections to stories and text in order to increase comprehension. Spend some time on each page of <u>Guess How Much I Love You</u> narrating the pictures. Tell your little one what is happening and make connections. You might link the text to other books, to personal experiences, or to events in the real world. On the page where Little Nutbrown Hare says, "I love you all the way up to my toes!", you might say:

> *Look at Little Nutbrown Hare. He is upside down. Where are his feet? Little Nutbrown Hare must really love Big Nutbrown Hare; he turned himself upside down to show how far away his toes are from his hands. Do you think that made Big Nutbrown Hare feel good? Mommies and daddies feel good when they know that their children love them. I love you very much, too, just like Little Nutbrown Hare and Big Nutbrown Hare love each other. I cannot hop as high as Big Nutbrown Hare. Do you think you can hop that high? I have other ways I can show you that I love you. I help you fall asleep, feed you, snuggle with you, read with you, and take care of you.*

As an extension, play the "I love you as much as/as far as/all the way to . . ." game, just like Little Nutbrown Hare and Big Nutbrown Hare. Making connections not only increases understanding, but also serves to honor your child's experiences, and helps your little one view stories through a personal lens.

Identify Physical Features

Teachers often point out familiar features of characters as they read books with young children. With your finger, point out identifying features of Little Nutbrown Hare and Big Nutbrown Hare in <u>Guess How Much I Love You</u>. For example, the hares have long ears, furry tails, twitching noses, soft fur, long legs, three-toed feet, little eyes, light spots, and smiling mouths. On the first page, you might say:

> *Look at Big Nutbrown Hare. He has two long ears. They are brown on the outside and pink on the inside. Big Nutbrown Hare also has a brown nose and long whiskers. Can you point to his whiskers? Look at his long feet. How many toes does Big Nutbrown Hare have? He also has a fluffy white tail. Can you point to his tail? Little Nutbrown Hare looks just like his daddy, but his body is much*

smaller. What else do you notice about Little Nutbrown Hare and Big Nutbrown Hare?

Point out as many features as you and your child can identify in each illustration.

Integrate Actions

Teachers use movement to enhance a book-sharing experience. Movement can also help active children access books. While you read Guess How Much I Love You, help your child understand the correlation between text and actions. First, ask your little one to point to Little Nutbrown Hare and Big Nutbrown Hare in each illustration. Then, describe what the hares are doing. Ask your little one to act out the motions. For example, on the page that says, "I love you as high as I can reach", you might say:

> *Look at Little Nutbrown Hare in this picture. He is standing up straight and reaching way up high with his little paws. Can you reach way up high? He is telling his daddy that he loves him as high as he can reach. Big Nutbrown Hare is standing up straight, too. His legs are spread apart, and he is reaching as high as he can. Can you stand like Big Nutbrown Hare? Little Nutbrown Hare is watching him with his arms and his ears down. What do you think Little Nutbrown Hare is thinking?*

As you read, ask your little one to demonstrate other actions and movements shown in the illustrations.

Vary Your Reading

Reading with emphasis, or changing the inflection and tone of your voice, helps draw children into the text. While reading Guess How Much I Love You, change your voice to represent the different characters. This will give your child a clearer understanding of who is speaking. For example, when Little Nutbrown Hare is speaking, you may decide to use a higher pitch, while Big Nutbrown Hare might inspire you to make your voice deeper. As you vary your voice, you and your little one can point to the character who is speaking. Changing your facial expressions and body language can work with a change in voice to communicate a different perspective.

Sing Along
Teachers know that the repetition and rhythm in songs help young children internalize new vocabulary. Use the text and illustrations on the pages of <u>Guess How Much I Love You</u> to spark a little song. You might sing "Here Comes Peter Cottontail" or "You Are My Sunshine". At the end of the story, when Little Nutbrown Hare goes to sleep, sing "Rock-a-bye Baby" or "Lullaby and Goodnight". Include any other songs or rhymes you and your little one can think of that are inspired by the illustrations or text.

Mr. Brown Can Moo! Can You?
Dr. Seuss's Book of Wonderful Noises
written and illustrated by Dr. Seuss

A journey into the wonderful sounds Mr. Brown
and the reader can make together
Features: clear, rhyming text that incorporates familiar sounds;
classic Dr. Seuss illustrations

Introduce Previewing

Teachers often preview books with children to activate their
thinking before a story even begins. Start by looking at the cover of
the book. Point to the title and cover picture. Talk about what you
might be thinking as you look at the cover. You might say:

*This story is called <u>Mr. Brown Can Moo! Can You?</u>. I
wonder what it could be about. The name* Mr. Brown *tells
me there is a man in the story. There is a picture of a man
right here, and his mouth is in an O shape. He is standing
with a cow. What do you think the man is doing? What do
you think the cow is going to do?*

Point out the name of the author and illustrator. You might say:

*This says, "Dr. Seuss's Book of Wonderful Noises." Dr.
Seuss is the author. He made up the story and wrote down
the words. Dr. Seuss is also the illustrator. He created the
pictures to go along with the words.*

Introduce Tracking

Black text on a white background provides a simple platform for helping young children learn that books have words that can be read (or tracked) from left to right. With your index finger, point to the words on the page as you read <u>Mr. Brown Can Moo! Can You?</u>. Start at the left and move slowly to the right and then down to the next line. Then, help your child track with his finger as you read. You might say:

> *When I read to you, I start on the left. Then, I read each word that comes next. When there are no more words to read on this line, I go down and start again on the next line. While we are reading this page, I am going to help you point to the words as I say each one.*

On some pages you and your little one might point to each word as you read, and on other pages sweep your fingers under the text without pausing on any particular word.

Recognize Letters and Words

Teachers use repetitive text to introduce young children to letters and words. Small words are powerful tools for emphasizing letter recognition and introducing the concept that individual letters strung together can create familiar words. Turn to the last two-page spread in <u>Mr. Brown Can Moo! Can You?</u>. Point to each set of words. Say each word, spell each word, and then say the word again. Be sure to point to the letters as you read and trace each letter with your finger. For example, as you point to the words *BUZZ BUZZ*, you might say:

> *Look at these two blue-green words. They say* BUZZ BUZZ. *B-U-Z-Z spells* BUZZ. BUZZ *starts with the letter* B. *This is the letter* B. *The capital letter* B *has one tall, straight line and two rounded lines. The letter* B *makes a buh sound. Buh, buh,* BUZZ. *Can you point to the word* BUZZ? *Do you see any other words on these pages that have a* B? *Yes, the words* DIBBLE DIBBLE *and* BOOM BOOM *also have Bs in them.*

Recognize Rhyming Words

Teachers know that there is a correlation between recognizing rhymes and reading readiness. Each two-page spread in <u>Mr. Brown Can Moo! Can You?</u> includes at least one rhyme. After you finish a page or verse that rhymes, help your child repeat the words that rhyme. Then, list additional words that rhyme. For example, on the first page, you might read:

> *"Oh, the wonderful sounds Mr. Brown can do! He can sound like a cow. He can go MOO MOO"*

Then, say:

> *On this page, the words* do *and* moo *rhyme. They both have the same* ooh *sound at the end. I wonder if we can think of other words that rhyme with* do *and* moo. *How about* boo? *Does* boo *end in the* ooh *sound? Can you think of another word that ends in the* ooh *sound?*

If your child suggests a word that rhymes but is not a real word, you can still support the process by saying:

> *Well done! The word you just made up has the* ooh *sound at the end. It rhymes with* do *and* moo.

Observe Picture Details

The background details in a picture contribute useful information about what is happening in a story. Teachers often ask children to notice details in the illustrations that may not be included in the text. Spend some time narrating Dr. Seuss's unique illustrations on each page of <u>Mr. Brown Can Moo! Can You?</u>. Talk with your little one about what you see and what is happening. For example, Mr. Brown's facial expressions and body language change with every sound he makes. His eyes are always closed, and near Mr. Brown's mouth are squiggly lines that reflect the sound being released. Point to Mr. Brown's face and the sounds he makes as you read. On the first page, you might say:

> *Look at Mr. Brown. He is saying MOO MOO. Look at his mouth. It is puckered in the shape of the ooooh sound. Can you make your mouth look like Mr. Brown's mouth? Can you make a moo sound, too? There are lines drawn near his mouth that show that he is mooing. Can you point to the lines? The cow is looking at Mr. Brown. It looks happy, and a bit surprised, that Mr. Brown is saying MOO.*

While you narrate, you and your little one can incorporate what you see, predict what you think might happen, ask questions, speak from personal experience, or even make up a story to go with the picture. Taking turns with your child while you are narrating is one strategy to encourage anticipation and idea sharing. You might start the narration on each page, then give your child a chance to contribute.

Consider Differences and Similarities

Teachers know that a basic understanding of comparisons is important for organizing ideas. Help your child conceptualize Dr. Seuss's unique versions of familiar objects by pointing out and labeling characters, animals, insects, plants, and objects in the pictures. For example, a horse or a rooster drawn by Dr. Seuss is sure to look different than a horse or a rooster in real life, or from any other toy or book your child has been exposed to before. Talk with your child about the differences between Dr. Seuss's pictures and pictures drawn in a more realistic way. On the page that says, "KLOPP KLOPP KLOPP", you might say:

> Dr. Seuss is the illustrator of _Mr. Brown Can Moo! Can You?_. Look at the way Dr. Seuss drew this horse. His horse is purple and has a short, spiky mane. It has a deeply swayed neck, and it smiles with its eyes closed. Are real horses purple? Most real horses have manes that are longer and necks that are straighter. Do you think a real horse would smile that wide?

If possible, show your little one a picture of a real horse and, together, point out the differences between the two images. As you read, point out any other similarities and differences you and your little one can find in the story.

Identify Colors, Patterns, and Shapes

Educators often ask young children to identify objects and patterns based on their colors and shapes. Dr. Seuss's illustrations contrast bright colors against white or solid backgrounds. As you share the pictures with your little one, point out and label the various colors, shapes, and patterns found in _Mr. Brown Can Moo! Can You?_, including details such as Mr. Brown's tie, the colors of the butterfly's wings, the different sounds on each page, and the color inside the clock. For example, on the page where Mr. Brown is buzzing, you might say:

> Look at these two bees. They have green wings, black-and-orange striped bodies, and long, black legs. What color are the mittens and booties they are wearing? Yes, they are orange. Both bees have two black antennae. What color are the tops of the antennae? Do you notice their circular shape?

You may decide to follow one object, pattern, or shape throughout the book or point out different features in each illustration.

Integrate Actions

Teachers use movement to enhance a book-sharing experience.
Movement can also help active children access books. While you
read <u>Mr. Brown Can Moo! Can You?</u>, help your child understand
the correlation between text and actions. First, ask your little one
to point to the animals and insects in each illustration. Then,
describe what they are doing. For example, the cow is smiling, the
bees are talking to each other, the bottle is popping, the horse is
walking, and the rain is falling. Ask your little one to act out the
motions. On the page with the goldfish, you might say:

> *Look at these two goldfish. They are in a fishbowl. The
> goldfish are swimming toward each other. What do you
> think will happen? Yes, their lips will touch. We can tell
> because their mouths are puckered close together. Look at
> my face. I am going to pucker my lips and blow you a kiss.
> Can you blow me a kiss? Why do you think the water is
> spilling out of their fishbowl, right above their heads? Yes,
> they must be swimming toward each other quickly. Can you
> show me what you would look like if you were swimming?*

As you read, ask your little one to demonstrate other actions and
movements shown in the illustrations.

Vary Your Reading

Reading with emphasis, or changing the inflection and tone of your
voice, helps draw children into the text. Whenever you read one of
the sounds in <u>Mr. Brown Can Moo! Can You?</u>, concentrate on
emphasizing the words and syllables, holding the sounds a little
longer than normal, using the range of your voice, reading louder
or softer depending on the sound, and experimenting with your
own vocal tones. For example, when you read "*BOOM BOOM
BOOM Mr. Brown is a wonder,*" you might read the words "*BOOM
BOOM BOOM*" with a stronger, more forceful tone. When you read
"*whisper whisper . . . very soft very high,*" drop your voice down to a
whisper. Changing your facial expressions and body language can
work with a change in voice to communicate a different
perspective. When you are finished reading, ask your child to say
"*BOOM BOOM BOOM*" in a forceful tone and "*whisper whisper*" in
a softer tone.

Sing Along
Teachers know that the repetition and rhythm in songs help young children internalize new vocabulary. Use the text and illustrations on the pages of <u>Mr. Brown Can Moo! Can You?</u> to spark a little song. On the pages with the cow or the horse, you might sing "Old MacDonald Had a Farm". On the page where Mr. Brown says "*pop, pop, pop, pop,*" sing "Pop! Goes the Weasel". To showcase more sounds, sing "The Wheels on the Bus Go 'Round and 'Round", concentrating on the sounds on the bus. Include any other songs or rhymes you and your little one can think of that are inspired by the illustrations or text.

The Dot
written and illustrated by Peter H. Reynolds

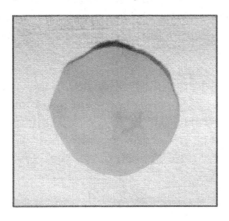

An inspiring journey from self-doubt to self-confidence
Features: hand lettered text; vibrant watercolor accents

Observe Picture Details

The background details in a picture contribute useful information about what is happening in a story. Teachers often ask children to notice details in the illustrations that may not be included in the text. Spend some time on each page of <u>The Dot</u> narrating the pictures. Talk with your little one about what you see and what is happening. For example, turn to the two-page spread when Vashti begins to paint a better dot than the one her teacher hung on the wall in art class. In the first image, point out that Vashti is sitting at a desk with her watercolors, a pencil, two different paint brushes, a bottle full of water, and several sheets of paper, each with one dot in the center. In the next picture, she has taped a larger piece of paper on the wall, moved her water jar to a stool, and has drawn several dots while experimenting with colors. Turning to the following page, you might say:

> Look, Vashti is on the floor now. She is drawing on a much larger sheet of paper. It is big enough for her body and her dot! What do you see next to her? What do you think is in the grey container by the wall? I think that is a container of water because when you paint with water colors you need to wet the paints to activate them — or get them to work. You also need to swirl your paintbrush in water so that it is

clean when you choose a new color. What colors do you think are in the two paint cans? Let's look at the dot. I see some yellow in her dot. Maybe one of the cans holds yellow paint. Do you think she is using a combination of water colors and regular paint? Why do you think she has two large paint brushes?

While you narrate, you and your little one can incorporate what you see, predict what you think might happen, ask questions, speak from personal experience, or even make up a story to go with the picture. Taking turns with your child while you are narrating is one strategy to encourage anticipation and idea sharing. You might start the narration on each page, then give your child a chance to contribute.

Introduce New Vocabulary
Teachers are aware that books often include vocabulary words that are unfamiliar to children. As a result, books often expose children to words they might not hear in everyday conversations. These words can give information, make a text sound more sophisticated or more like everyday speech, or help convey emotion. After you have read <u>The Dot</u> and your little one is familiar with the story, you may want to explain these words: *gazing, swirly, glued, grabbed, jab, hmmph, discovered, experimented,* and *splashed.* One way that educators explain these words is to add familiar words with similar meanings as they read. For example, when Vashti meets the little boy at the art show, you might say:
> *This says that the little boy was "gazing" — or looking — "up at her." Why do you think the author chose the word gazing instead of just saying looking or staring? I think he chose gazing so you would know that he was looking at her carefully and steadily and admiring her. Can you show me how you would gaze up at me? I am going to gaze at you, too.*

On the page with Vashti's artwork framed on the wall, you might say:
> *This page says that Vashti's dot was "All framed in swirly" — or curved — "gold." Why do you think the author chose the word swirly? Yes, I think it was to let you know that the frame was not just gold and straight. Do you see the rounded and wavy parts of the frame in the picture? I also*

*think he knows that swirly is an adjective that kids
sometimes use. Can you make a swirly motion with your
hand?*

Making connections to stories is a tool that educators use to
encourage critical thinking. If you come across these words in
other books you share, or in another setting, remind your child
that you also saw them in <u>The Dot</u>.

Consider Word Choice

Authors sometimes use idioms or common colloquial phrases to
add charm and character to their text. Teachers know that while
these phrases are fun to read and make sense in the context of the
book, they often need to be explained to young children. In <u>The
Dot</u>, Peter H. Reynolds includes phrases such as: "glued to her
chair", "a polar bear in a snowstorm", "set to work", "made quite a
splash", and "I can't draw a straight line with a ruler". Explain
some of these fun word choices to your little one. For example, on
the page where Vashti is sitting in the classroom by herself, you
might say:

*This says that Vashti sat "glued to her chair." That sounds
funny! Why do we use glue? Yes, to stick things in one
place. Do you think she is really glued to her chair? I do not
think so either. What specific idea about the way she was
sitting in her chair is the author trying to give you by using
the word glued? Yes, she was not lounging, she was not
moving to get up, she was not wiggling; she was sitting very
still in one spot.*

On the page where the teacher looks at Vashti's empty paper, you
might say:

*What do you see when you look at Vashti's paper? To me,
this looks like a clean, empty piece of paper without a mark
on it. Vashti did not draw anything at all, but the teacher
tells Vashti that her all white piece of paper looks like a
"polar bear in a snow storm." What do you think that
means? Polar bears are white animals that live in cold
climates. Snow is white too, so if a polar bear was in a
swirling snowstorm you would not really be able to see it.
Everything would look white. Why do you think the teacher
said that? Yes, she was making a joke. I think she said it to
try to make Vashti laugh a little and feel less upset because*

she was hoping to encourage Vashti to try again. I like that the author did not just have the teacher say: "you did not draw anything." Do you think that was a good choice?

Recognize Expressions and Emotions

Illustrators often vary a character's expressions or body language in order to convey a particular emotion. In <u>The Dot</u>, Vashti's eyes, mouth, and body language are very expressive. Her emotions are further illustrated by the watercolors that frame her in certain images. Explain to your little one that the reader can tell what Vashti is feeling by looking carefully at how her eyes and body change in each picture, and what colors surround her. For example, on the page where Vashti "gives the paper a good, strong jab", you might say:

Vashti seems really upset in this picture. She does not think she can draw and her teacher asked her to make a mark. I can tell Vashti is upset because the story says she jabbed her marker against the paper. A jab is much stronger than a gentle mark. Do you ever feel upset when someone asks you to do something you do not want to do? Look at how Vashti is sitting in her chair. Yes, she is sitting backwards. She is not facing her paper, so she has to turn her body around to make her mark. Let's look at Vashti's eyes. Her eyebrows are drawn at a slant, so I know she has furrowed her brow [show your little one a furrowed brow]. *Can you furrow your brow? I also notice that Vashti is surrounded by colors. What colors do you notice? Yes, red and orange. Red is often used to illustrate anger. The red water colors seem to reflect Vashti's angry and frustrated mood.*

Next, turn to the two-page spread where all of Vashti's dots are on display at the school art show. You might say:

Look at Vashti now. She is holding her drawing pad in a gentle way and looking at a sculpture. Her mouth is turned up. Do you think she looks happy? What color is Vashti surrounded by now? Yes, yellow! Yellow is a color often used to illustrate happiness or content. Look at the other people on the page. They all look happy, too. They are smiling and enjoying Vashti's artwork. This is what my face looks like when I am smiling and happy [show your little one your smile]. *Can you show me your happy face? Why do you think Vashti is so happy on this page?*

Predict and Pretend

Teachers often ask children to predict, pretend, ask questions, and think critically while they are reading. These are important tools for comprehension and advanced interaction between the reader and a book. As you read <u>The Dot</u>, expose your little one to language and interactive thoughts by modeling these tools. For example, on the very last page, Vashti asks the boy to sign his name after drawing a squiggly line. Looking at the picture, you might say:

Look at the boy. Vashti is asking him to sign his name. He looks like he cannot believe she wants his signature. What do you think will happen next? Do you think Vashti will hang his drawing in a fancy frame? Remember when Vashti's teacher hung her first dot in a swirly gold frame? Do you think the boy will see the frame and feel inspired to draw many kinds of squiggly lines? He could hang all his artwork just like Vashti did. I wonder if he will inspire someone else to draw. Or maybe they will draw a picture together. Should we draw a picture together?

It is important to note that there is no right answer to these questions. The idea is to help your child learn to think aloud and practice critical thinking. While you predict and pretend, notice how prior knowledge and past experiences influence your conversation. You might also tell your child about something you dreamed about doing when you were a child.

Make Connections

Educators ask children to make connections to stories and text in order to increase comprehension. Spend some time on each page of <u>The Dot</u> narrating the pictures. Tell your little one what is happening and make connections. You might link the text to other books, to personal experiences, or to events in the real world. For example, on the page where Vashti jabs the marker onto the paper, you might say:

In this part of the story, Vashti jabs the marker onto the paper. I think she is feeling frustrated because she thinks she cannot draw. I do not think she would have jabbed the marker onto the paper if she was feeling calm. How do you act when you are frustrated? Sometimes when I am frustrated I get a bit grumpy, just like Vashti. I get especially frustrated when I am having trouble doing something, if I am running late, or if I drop and break what I am holding. What is something that might make you feel frustrated? It is very normal to feel frustrated because sometimes things are hard. We have to always remember that trying is important.

On the page where Vashti discovers that blue and yellow make green, you might say:

Vashti is mixing colors together. Have you ever mixed colors together? When you mix the color blue and the color yellow, you can make green. I loved to make green with paints when I was little. I also loved to mix blue and red. Do you know what color you can make by mixing blue and red? Right, purple. What is your favorite color right now? Blue was my favorite color when I was young, so I loved to use it as much as I could. If I were Vashti, all my dots would have blue in them. What color dots would you make?

Making connections not only increases understanding, but also serves to honor your child's experiences, and helps your little one view stories through a personal lens.

Consider Differences and Similarities

Teachers know that a basic understanding of comparisons is important for organizing ideas. Use Peter H. Reynold's illustrations to highlight differences and similarities in The Dot. On many of the pages, the background includes a dot surrounding Vashti. These dots are different colors throughout the book. Open to the pages showing the teacher studying Vashti's first dot and asking her to sign it. You might say:

Look at the illustrations on these pages. What do you notice about the colors? Yes, the teacher and the paper are drawn in black and white and grey.

Then, turn the page to show Vashti signing her name. You might say:

Now, look at this page. What do you see in this picture that is a bit different? Yes, Vashti and the paper are still drawn in black and white and grey, but there is an orange dot surrounding her. Do you know what two colors you can mix to make orange? Yes, red and yellow.

The color of the dot surrounding Vashti changes as the story progresses. Show your child the way the dot around Vashti looks on different pages and ask your child to point out the different colors. You might say:

Look, the dot around Vashti is different on each page. What color is the dot at the beginning of the story, when she is angry? Yes, the dot is red and dark. On this page, when Vashti is creating, what do you notice? Yes, the dot is made up of several colors. Why do you think the illustrator changes the color of the dot? I think the illustrator wants to give you a different feeling when he changes the color of the dot.

Toward the end, there is a dot around the boy Vashti is inspiring as he draws his line. Focus on the similarity between the dot surrounding him, and the dot surrounding Vashti on the page where she stands next to the stool and experiments with many colors. You might say:

Look at this beautiful, colored dot around the boy when Vashti is helping him discover what he can do. Does it remind you of another dot in the story? It reminds me of the dot around Vashti when she was discovering what she could do. How do these dots make you feel? I think they are very similar and I have a similar nice feeling when I look at them.

A special difference between this book and others is that Peter H. Reynolds uses his own handwriting as the typeset. On the first page of the story, show your child the words on the page. You might say:

Look at these words; how do they look different from the words in some of the other books we read together? Yes, they look like regular writing. All the words in this book were written by the author with a pen or marker, instead of typed on a typewriter or computer. Why do you think he decided to do that? Maybe it was to make the words and the drawings look even more connected.

As you read, point out any other similarities and differences you find in the story. When you read other books by Peter H. Reynolds, you can remind your child about <u>The Dot</u> having had similar handwriting text.

Teachable Moment

Often, picture books include an important message, or a moral, that resonates with young children. Teachers use these stories to reinforce specific behaviors, teach about right and wrong, or introduce a new lesson. There are several themes in <u>The Dot</u> that are relevant to children and adults alike. Exploring your own creativity, bravely overcoming self-doubt, finding self-confidence, building momentum, and inspiring others are all ways to "make your mark". Talk with your little one about these themes as you read. For example, on the page where the young boy is gazing up at Vashti at the art show, you might say:

> *Look at this little boy. He is excited by Vashti's dots at the school art show. He is gazing up at her. He thinks she is a wonderful artist. The little boy does not know that at the beginning of the story Vashti was upset and frustrated. She did not think she could draw anything at all. Remember what her teacher said? Yes, her teacher told her to "just make a mark and see where it takes you." Vashti began with one tiny dot and built momentum. Do you know what momentum is? She kept making more and more dots in new and creative ways. The more dots she made, the easier it became for her to explore and create. Now she has a whole wall full of art and feels happy and proud of herself. I am very proud of who you are becoming, too. Do you ever feel proud of yourself?*

As you finish the story, you might say:

> *The little boy is just like Vashti at the beginning of the story. He does not think he can draw either. He was so nervous when he was drawing a line that his hand was shaking. Look at his line. It came out all squiggly. What did Vashti ask him to do after she looked at his artwork? Yes, she asked him to sign his name on the paper, just like her teacher told her to sign her name when she drew her first dot. Do you think Vashti has changed now that she has her dots? I think that instead of feeling worried about art, she is inspiring the little boy to feel brave and make his own mark!*

Identify Colors, Patterns, and Shapes

Educators often ask young children to identify objects and patterns based on their colors and shapes. Peter H. Reynold's illustrations in The Dot are vibrant and detailed. As you share the pictures with your little one, point out various colors, shapes, and patterns. For example, in the middle of the story, there is a two-page spread showing Vashti's work displayed at the art show. Help your little one point to each canvas on the wall and name the shapes. You might say:

> Vashti has a lot of canvases on this wall of the art show. They are different sizes and shapes. Some of her canvases are long rectangles and some are a kind of rectangle that is called a square. Let's point to each of the canvases and you and I can name the shape: square ... rectangle ... rectangle ... square ... [etc.] Some of the rectangles are long and narrow. Others are wider. They are hung in different ways, but they are all still rectangles. Can you point to the largest rectangle? It takes up a great deal of room on the wall. Let's look at Vashti's dots. Dots are a shape called a circle. Can you point to a few circles?

Then, ask your little one to point to the colored dots on each canvas and name the color. You might say:

> The dots Vashti has painted are all different colors. Let's name some of the colors of the dots we see. This dot is all white. Vashti painted with green and blue around the large canvas, so the middle is a white circle. What color is this dot? Yes, it is yellow. How about this one? Yes, it is green and yellow. This dot has several colors in it. Can you name some of the other colors you see on this page? Some of the dots even have designs inside of them. I am trying to decide which dot is my favorite. Which one is your favorite?

You may decide to follow one object, pattern, or shape throughout the book or point out different features in each illustration.

Practice Number Sense

Books provide a platform for introducing the concept of number sense and exposing children to an early visual understanding of math. Use the pages of The Dot to play counting games. Pointing to the opening page, you might say:

Look at Vashti's classroom. There are tables and chairs in the room. I wonder how many tables there are. Let's count them together: one, two, three tables. I wonder how many chairs there are. Let's count them together: one, two, three, four, five, six, seven, and the one she is sitting on makes eight. [Pause to let your child provide the next number in the sequence if he is able.] *Do you think there are more chairs and tables in the classroom that we cannot see? I also see four items on the table where Vashti is sitting: paper, a paintbrush, a pencil, and her box of watercolors.*

Next turn to the page where Vashti opens her watercolor box. You might say:

Look, Vashti's watercolor box is open. Let's count how many colors are in it: one, two, three, four, five, six colors. [Pause to let your child provide the next number in the sequence if he is able.] *What else do you see? Yes, she has a few pieces of paper. How many are there? Let's count them: one, two, three. She still has one pencil and one paintbrush.*

As you read, count how many dots are on a page, how many fingers you see, how many pieces of paper Vashti has, or how many buckets of paint are on the floor. Count anything else that you and your little one can find in the illustrations.

Vary Your Reading

Reading with emphasis, or changing the inflection and tone of your voice, helps draw children into the text. While reading <u>The Dot</u>, change your voice to represent the different characters. This will help give your child a clear understanding of who is speaking. For example, when the teacher is speaking, you may decide to use a lower pitch, while Vashti might inspire you to make your voice a little higher. As you vary your voice, point to the character who is speaking. You can also ask your child to point to the character as you read. Changing your facial expressions and body language can work with a change in voice to communicate a different perspective.

Sing Along

Teachers know that the repetition and rhythm in songs help young children internalize new vocabulary. Use the text and illustrations on the pages of <u>The Dot</u> to spark a little song. You might sing "The

Dot Song", "Somewhere Over the Rainbow", "The Rainbow Connection", or "This Little Light of Mine". Include any other songs or rhymes you and your little one can think of that are inspired by the illustrations or text.

Corduroy
written and illustrated by Don Freeman

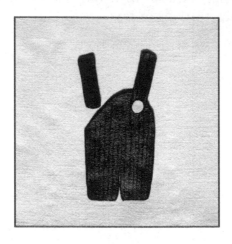

Classic book about a bear living in a department store, hoping for a real home
Features: engaging, narrative text; ink and watercolor illustrations

Recognize Letters and Words

Teachers use repetitive text to introduce young children to letters and words. Small words are powerful tools for emphasizing letter recognition and introducing the concept that individual letters strung together can create familiar words. Every time the word *button* appears in <u>Corduroy</u>, point to it, say it, spell it, and then say it again. You might say:

> *This is the word* button. *The letters* b-u-t-t-o-n *spell* button. *Look, here is the word* button *again.* Button *begins with the letter* B. *Buh, buh,* B. *A capital* B *is a letter made with one straight line and two curved lines. We can find the word* button *on many pages of this book. Buh, buh,* button. *Can you point to the word* button *on this page? Can you help me say the letters in the word* button?

Point to the letters as you say each one together and trace each letter with your finger. As you continue reading, pause before reading the word *button* to see if your child can fill in the word. To further illustrate the relationship between words and pictures, ask your child to point to the button in the illustrations.

Recognize Expressions and Emotions

Illustrators often vary a character's expressions or body language in order to convey a particular emotion. The characters in <u>Corduroy</u> are very expressive. Explain how you can tell what the characters are feeling by looking carefully at the illustrations. For example, on the page where Lisa is leaving the department store with her mother, you might say:

> *Lisa is walking out of the store, but Corduroy has to stay. How do you think they are feeling? I think they are sad, too. Their mouths are turned down and Lisa's eyebrows are going up a little. I think they are sad because they really wanted to be together, but Lisa could not buy Corduroy.*

Later, when Lisa runs up the stairs with Corduroy, you might say:

> *Do you think Lisa and Corduroy are feeling happy now? Yes, Lisa has a big smile on her face. Also, it looks like she is running as fast as she can. Sometimes people have a lot of energy when they are excited or happy.*

On the last page, you might say:

> *I think Corduroy is happy that Lisa brought him home. Can you tell why I think that? Yes, Corduroy is smiling and snuggling with Lisa when she hugs him.*

As you read, mimic the expressions of the characters. You might say:

> *This is how I look when I am excited like Lisa* [express excitement]. *Can you show me how you look when you are excited?*

Predict and Pretend

Teachers often ask children to predict, pretend, ask questions, and think critically while they are reading. These are important tools for comprehension and advanced interaction between the reader and a book. As you read <u>Corduroy</u>, expose your little one to language and interactive thoughts by modeling these tools. For example, after reading the page where the security guard says, "How did *you* get upstairs?" think aloud about why Corduroy is searching so hard for his lost button. You might say:

> *Corduroy has been searching all over the store for his missing button. Why do you think it is important for Corduroy to find his button? Yes, because he heard Lisa's mother mention that his button was missing. That was one*

of the reasons they did not buy him. He must really want someone to take him home. It looks like Corduroy climbed under the covers. Do you think he was looking for his button in the bed or was he hiding from the night watchman?

It is important to note that there is no right answer to these questions. The idea is to help your child learn to think aloud and practice critical thinking. While you predict and pretend, notice how prior knowledge and past experiences influence your conversation.

Make Connections

Educators ask children to make connections to stories and text in order to increase comprehension. Spend some time on each page of Corduroy narrating the pictures. Tell your little one what is happening and make connections. You might link the text to other books, to personal experiences, or to events in the real world. For example, on the page where Corduroy first sees Lisa's room, you might say:

Look, Corduroy is in Lisa's room. I see a lot of objects in her room that look familiar. She is kneeling down next to a black rocking chair with a pink cushion. I used to have a rocking chair in my home when I was growing up. I loved to sit in the rocking chair and read books. Look at the flower pot on her windowsill. Do we have flowers in our home? Here is Lisa's bed. Do you sleep in a bed? What else do you see that you recognize?

Making connections not only increases understanding, but also serves to honor your child's experiences, and helps your little one view stories through a personal lens.

Consider Differences and Similarities

Teachers know that a basic understanding of comparisons is important for organizing ideas. Use Don Freeman's illustrations to highlight the differences and similarities in Corduroy. First, point out Corduroy and the white rabbit on the first page. You might say:

Look, Corduroy is right next to the white rabbit. They are both stuffed animals. Corduroy and the white rabbit both have two eyes, a nose, a mouth, ears, paws, and soft fur.

How are the bunny rabbit and Corduroy different? Yes, the
white rabbit is sitting on the shelf, while Corduroy is
standing. Corduroy has brown fur, and the rabbit has
white fur. The rabbit's eyes are pink, and he has whiskers.
The white rabbit is also much bigger than Corduroy and is
wearing only a blue bow, while Corduroy wears overalls.

Together with your little one, point out any other features that are
similar or different. You might even compare all the toys on the
shelf. For example, the giraffe has much longer legs than the
rabbit, and the rabbit has much longer ears. As you read, point out
any other similarities and differences you and your little one can
find in the story.

Identify Physical Features

Teachers often point out familiar features of characters as they
read books with young children. With your finger, point out the
identifying features of each toy in <u>Corduroy</u>. For example, the bear
has fuzzy brown fur and is wearing green overalls. The giraffe has
a long neck and brown spots. The bunny has two long ears. The
clown has a red nose and striped pants. The turtle is green and has
a shell. On the first page, you might say:

Look at the giraffe on the shelf next to Corduroy. It has a
long neck, long eyelashes, and long ears. What color are the
spots on its body? How many horns does the giraffe have on
the top of its head?

Point out as many features as you and your child can identify in
each illustration.

Identify Colors, Patterns, and Shapes

Educators often ask young children to identify objects and patterns
based on their colors and shapes. The illustrations in <u>Corduroy</u> are
enlivened with bold watercolors. As you share the pictures with
your little one, point out the various colors, shapes, and patterns.
For example, on the first page, you might say:

Look at Corduroy. He is wearing green overalls. His fur is
brown. The bunny is next to Corduroy. The bunny's fur is
white. What color is the bunny's bow? The doll on the shelf
is wearing a pink dress with a blue sash.

On the page where Corduroy steps off the escalator, you might say:

Look at the lamps. Many of the lampshades are drawn as trapezoids. A trapezoid is a shape with four sides, with one pair of opposite sides that are parallel. Each lampshade is a different color. What color lampshades do you see?

In Lisa's room, point out the green overalls again, then say:

Let's see if we can find something else that is green in Lisa's room. These stripes are green; they are on the wall.

You can also find shapes in Lisa's room. As you read, you might say:

The rug is round; it is a circle. Can you use your finger to trace the circle? The end of Corduroy's new bed is a rectangle. Can you trace the rectangle with your finger? The picture frame is a rectangle, too. What else do you see that is a rectangle?

You may decide to follow one object, pattern, or shape throughout the book or point out different features in each illustration.

Practice Number Sense

Books provide a platform for introducing the concept of number sense and exposing children to an early visual understanding of math. Use the pages of Corduroy to play counting games. For example, on the page with the tables, chairs, and beds, you might say:

There is a lot of furniture on this page. I see couches, chairs, tables, beds, and lamps in this big room. Help me count the beds: one, two, three, four, five, six, seven, eight, nine beds. [Pause to let your child provide the next number in the sequence if he is able.] *Is there a pillow on each bed? Yes, that means there are nine bed pillows, too. How many beds are there in our home? I wonder how many lamps there are in this picture. Let's count the lamps: one, two, three, four, five, six, seven, eight, nine, ten, eleven, twelve. There are twelve lamps. Are there more lamps in the room or more beds? Yes, there are more lamps than beds in this room.*

As you read, help your child count toys, hats on the characters, steps on the escalator, various types of furniture, buttons on the different characters' clothing, or anything else you find in the illustrations.

Vary Your Reading

Reading with emphasis, or changing the inflection and tone of your voice, helps draw children into the text. While reading <u>Corduroy</u>, emphasize passages with question marks or exclamation points by adjusting your voice and tone. For example, when you come to words like *mountain, pop, bang, crash, gasped,* and *cried,* use variations in your voice to convey the sounds and actions. After your initial few readings, pause so that your child can supply the word with enthusiasm. Changing your facial expressions and body language can work with a change in voice to communicate a different perspective.

Sing Along

Teachers know that the repetition and the rhythm in songs help young children internalize new vocabulary. Use the text and illustrations on the pages of <u>Corduroy</u> to inspire a little song. You might sing "Teddy Bears' Picnic", "If You're Happy and You Know It", "There's a Hole in the Bucket", "The Bear Went Over the Mountain", or "The More We Get Together". Include any other songs or rhymes you and your little one can think of that are inspired by the text or illustrations.

Goodnight Moon
written by Margaret Wise Brown,
illustrated by Clement Hurd

Classic goodnight story first published in 1947
Features: colorful pictures, contrasted with black-and-white images

Introduce New Vocabulary
Teachers are aware that books often include vocabulary words or images that may be unfamiliar to children. Goodnight Moon was first published in 1947. The room in the story reflects this time period. Point out some of the notable items in the room, such as the corded phone, the drying rack, the two antique clocks, the copy of Goodnight Moon on the nightstand, the fire irons, the extra wood for the fireplace, the baby bunny's slippers, and anything else you and your child find interesting. After each full-color spread, there is a black-and-white close-up picture of some of the items in the room. Talk with your little one about the black-and-white images. For example, on the page with the comb, brush, and bowl, you might say:

> *Look at the bowl with the spoon. This is a bowl full of mush. We do not typically call our food mush anymore. What do you think the mush is? I think it might be oatmeal, cream of wheat, porridge, cornmeal, or grits.*

Making connections to stories is a tool that educators use to encourage critical thinking. If you come across these words or items in other books you share, or in another setting, remind your child that you also saw them in Goodnight Moon.

Recognize Letters and Words

Teachers use repetitive text to introduce young children to letters and words. Small words are powerful tools for emphasizing letter recognition and introducing the concept that individual letters strung together can create familiar words. Every time the word *goodnight* appears in <u>Goodnight Moon</u>, point to it, say it, spell it, and then say it again. You might say:

> *This is the word* goodnight. *The letters* g-o-o-d-n-i-g-h-t *spell* goodnight. *Look, here is the word* goodnight *again.* Goodnight *begins with the letter* G. *The letter* G *makes two sounds; in this word, the letter* G *makes a* guh *sound. Guh, guh,* goodnight. *We can find the word* goodnight *on many pages of this book. Can you point to the word* goodnight *on this page? Can you help me say the letters in the word* goodnight?

Point to the letters as you say each one together and trace each letter with your finger. As you continue reading, pause before reading the word *goodnight* to see if your child can fill in the word.

Observe Picture Details

The background details in a picture contribute useful information about what is happening in a story. Teachers often ask children to notice details in the illustrations that may not be included in the text. Spend some time on each page of <u>Goodnight Moon</u> narrating the pictures. Tell your little one what you see and what is happening. For example, when you open to the picture of the fireplace on the first page, point out the flames and the logs, the tools in the stand, the log holder, the mantle, the clock, and the other mantle decorations. You might say:

> *The flames of the fire are reaching high inside the fireplace. Maybe they just added some new wood to the fire. Can you point to where they keep the wood they will add to the fire next? Do you see the tools they use to tend the fire? They might use those tools to move the logs or scoop up the ashes. Why do you think there is a fire lit in the room right now? The shelf above the fireplace is called a mantle. What do you see on the mantle?*

While you narrate, you and your little one can incorporate what you see, predict what you think might happen, ask questions, speak from personal experience, or even make up a story to go with the picture. Taking turns with your child while you are narrating is one strategy to encourage anticipation and idea sharing. You might start the narration on each page, then give your child a chance to contribute.

Consider Differences and Similarities
Teachers know that a basic understanding of comparisons is important for organizing ideas. Use Clement Hurd's illustrations to highlight differences and similarities in <u>Goodnight Moon</u>. For example, some of the illustrations are full-color, while others are black-and-white. On some pages, the colors are different, but the illustrations are exactly the same. On other pages, the black-and-white pictures are slightly different from the colorful spreads. Point out specific features that make each picture the same and the features in each picture that are different. On the black-and-white page highlighting the quiet old lady, you might say:

> Look at the quiet old lady whispering hush. She is knitting in a rocking chair. Her yarn is in a ball at her feet. Can you tell what color her yarn is? We cannot tell because the picture has been drawn without bright colors. Let's turn the page. There is the quiet old lady again. She looks exactly the same except that we can see more color now. What color is her ball of yarn? Yes, it is green. Is it still at her feet? Who is playing with the yarn? The yarn looks different. It has rolled onto the rug, and the kittens are playing with it.

Next, point out the changes in the room as it becomes darker. For example, when the little bunny first goes to bed it is 7:00 PM; by the end of the book, it is 8:00 PM and considerably darker. You might say:

> Now that we are at the end of the story, can you see how the fire seems brighter in the darker room? Look at the moon and the lights in the miniature house; they are also different from how they were at the beginning of the story. What else do you notice?

As you read, point out any other similarities and differences you and your little one can find in the story.

Consider the Movement of the Earth and the Moon
Teachers often use books to illustrate basic scientific concepts. The illustrations in <u>Goodnight Moon</u> introduce the concept of moonrise.

On the first page there is no moon in the window. On the next full-color spread, the moon is visible in the bottom left corner of the window near the rocking chair. As the story continues, a little more of the moon appears. The same way the sun rises in the east and moves across the sky to set in the west — highest above us in the middle of the day, and closest to the horizon when it first appears and right before it sets — the moon crosses the sky at night. This happens because Earth is always turning on its axis while it revolves around the sun, and the moon revolves around the earth. Point out the continued reveal of the moon in each full-color spread. You might say:

> On the first page, the bunny is in bed and there are stars outside the window. Do you see the moon? Let's see if we can find the moon on the next page with a window. Do you see a tiny bit of the moon peeking through in the left hand corner of a window? I notice that each time we turn the page, a little bit more of the moon is visible. That is because our planet, Earth, is always slowly turning and the moon revolves — or circles — around Earth. This makes it look like the moon is traveling across the sky. Can you find the picture where the moon looks the largest? The bunny has a nice view of the moon from the bed. Do you think the bunny says goodnight to the moon even when it is cloudy outside?

The next time you see the moon in the sky, point it out to your child and mention Goodnight Moon.

Identify Animals

To help build vocabulary and expose your little one to animals and their features, name each animal in the bedroom in Goodnight Moon. As you turn the pages, point to all the animals you see in the illustrations, including animals in the pictures on the wall. Identify each animal, point out any distinguishing features, and make its sound. For example, on the page that says, "Goodnight room", you might say:

> Look at all the animals in the bunny's room. I see a yellow stuffed giraffe here at the top of the bookshelf. Its neck is very long so it can reach delicious leaves high up in the trees. What other animals do you see on the bookshelf? Yes, I see an elephant sitting at the bottom of the bookshelf, too. It is grey and shorter than the giraffe. The elephant's trunk

is long, so it can pick up food to put in its mouth. Look at the two kittens playing with the yarn. They look alike except for their colors. One is dark, and one is light. What sound do kittens make? Do you see the little mouse? Let's try to find the little mouse on some of the other pages.

See if your child can find all the animals in the room.

Identify Colors, Patterns, and Shapes

Educators often ask young children to identify objects and patterns based on their colors and shapes. The illustrations in <u>Goodnight Moon</u> alternate between color and black-and-white. On the colorful pages, the illustrator, Clement Hurd, uses bold colors — sometimes solid, sometimes in stripes — and a few patterns and designs. As you share the pictures with your little one, point out various colors, shapes, and patterns. Include the different colors and designs on objects in the room and the background colors of the walls and floor. For example, on the first page, you might say:

Look at the balloon. It is a bright red circle. Can you find other red objects on this page? Yes, the bed, the rug, the bowl, the fire, the window frame, and the barns in the picture above the fireplace are all red. The blanket is orange. It is a triangle with three sides. Can you use your finger to trace the triangle? I notice other shapes in this illustration. The windows in the miniature house each have four sides. They are rectangles. Where else do you see rectangles in the room? The rug is a circular shape. I also notice stars in the sky. Can you point to them?

You may decide to follow one object, pattern, or shape throughout the book or point out different features in each illustration.

Practice Number Sense

Books provide a platform for introducing the concept of number sense and exposing children to an early visual understanding of math. Use the pages of <u>Goodnight Moon</u> to play counting games. For example, on the page that says, "And there were three little bears sitting on chairs", you might say:

Look, there are bears on this page. Can you help me count the bears? One, two, three. They are sitting on chairs. Let's count the chairs, too: one, two, three. Are there the same number of bears and chairs? Each bear has two ears. Let's

count all the ears: one, two, three, four, five, six ears.
[Pause to let your child provide the next number in the
sequence if he is able.] *I can also count by twos: two, four,
six ears.*

Together with your little one, find and count one cow, two kittens,
three bears, four mittens, and five windows in the miniature
house. Count anything else you and your child find in the
illustrations.

Vary Your Reading

Reading with emphasis, or changing the inflection and tone of your
voice, helps draw children into the text. While reading Goodnight
Moon, vary your voice each time you read the word *goodnight*. For
example, when you read: "Goodnight light and the red balloon . . .
Goodnight bears . . . Goodnight chairs," use a different pitch, and a
softer tone when reading *Goodnight* and your regular voice when
reading the rest. Changing your facial expressions and body
language can work with a change in voice to communicate a
different perspective.

Sing Along

Teachers know that the repetition and rhythm in songs help young
children internalize new vocabulary. Use the text and illustrations
on the pages of Goodnight Moon to spark a little song. On the page
with the bunny, you might sing "Here Comes Peter Cottontail",
"Little Peter Rabbit", or "Do Your Ears Hang Low?". When you
turn to the page with the bunny snug in bed, sing a little song to
help the bunny sleep. You might sing "Rock-a-bye Baby" or
"Lullaby and Goodnight". When you look at the cow jumping over
the moon, you might sing "Cat's in the Cradle" or recite the rhyme
"Hickory Dickory Dock". Include any other songs or rhymes you
and your little one can think of that are inspired by the
illustrations or text.

Baby Cakes
written by Karma Wilson, illustrated by Sam Williams

Sweet, rhyming interaction between babies and their teddy bear
Features: large, soft pictures incorporating many different babies

Introduce Previewing

Teachers often preview books with children to activate their
thinking before a story even begins. Start by looking at the cover of
the book. Point to the title and picture. Talk about what you might
be thinking as you look at the cover. You might say:

> *This story is called* <u>Baby Cakes</u>; *what do you think it could
> be about? Does the word* Baby *in the title give you a hint?
> Who is in the picture? What ideas does that give you about
> what might happen in the story?*

Point out the name of the author and illustrator. You might say:

> *Karma Wilson is the author. She made up the story and
> wrote down the words. Sam Williams is the illustrator. He
> created the pictures to go along with the words.*

Before the title page is a two-page illustration of a teddy bear with
a ball and a baby walking. Ask your child what she thinks these
pictures will have to do with the story.

Recognize Letters and Words

Teachers use repetitive text to introduce young children to letters
and words. Small words are powerful tools for emphasizing letter
recognition and introducing the concept that individual letters
strung together can create familiar words. Every time the word

baby appears in <u>Baby Cakes</u>, point to it, say it, spell it, and then say it again. You might say:

> *This book is called* <u>Baby Cakes</u>. *This is the word* Baby. *The letters* b-a-b-y *spell* baby. *Look, here is the word* baby *again.* Baby *begins with the letter* B. *Buh, buh,* B. *The lowercase letter* b *has a tall straight line and a small curved line. We can find the word* baby *on many pages of this book. Buh, buh,* baby. *Can you point to the word* baby *on this page? Can you help me say the letters in the word* baby?

Point to the letters as you say each one together and trace each letter with your finger. As you continue reading, pause before reading the word *baby* to see if your child can fill in the word. To further illustrate the relationship between words and pictures, ask your child to point to the baby in the illustrations.

Recognize Rhyming Words

Teachers know that there is a correlation between recognizing rhymes and reading readiness. Every other sentence in <u>Baby Cakes</u> includes a rhyme. After you finish a page or verse that rhymes, help your child repeat the words that rhyme. Then, list additional words that rhyme. For example, on the page with the red wagon in the text box, you might read:

> *"Nibble little Baby Cakes on the feet. Oh, my little Baby Cakes tastes so sweet!"*

Then, say:

> *On this page, the words* feet *and* sweet *rhyme. They both have the same* eet *sound at the end. I wonder if we can think of other words that rhyme with* feet *and* sweet? *How about* treat? *Does* treat *end in the* eet *sound? Can you think of another word that ends in the* eet *sound?*

If your child suggests a word that rhymes but is not a real word, you can still support the process by saying:

> *Well done! The word you just made up has the* eet *sound at the end. It rhymes with* feet *and* sweet.

Identify Physical Features

Teachers often point out familiar features of characters as they read books with young children. With your finger, point out and name identifying features of the boy and the teddy bear in <u>Baby</u>

Cakes. For example, the bear and the boy have some matching features, such as eyes, ears, rosy cheeks, mouths, and posture. On the page that says, "Tickle little Baby Cakes. Gooch-a-goo!", you might say:

> *Look at the baby and the bear. Do you think they are happy? Yes, they are both giggling. It looks like the baby is reaching out to tickle the bear. I see five fingers on one of the baby's hands. I cannot see the baby's toes. Does the bear have fingers or toes? Can you point to their eyes? Their eyes are both closed a little because they are laughing. This is what I look like when I am happy.* [express happiness] *Can you show me what you look like when you are happy?*

Point out as many features as you and your little one can identify in each illustration.

Identify Colors, Patterns, and Shapes

Educators often ask young children to identify objects and patterns based on their colors and shapes. Sam Williams uses many colors in his pictures — sometimes solid, sometimes in stripes — and a few patterns and designs. As you share the pictures in Baby Cakes with your little one, point out various colors, patterns, and shapes, including the small picture and the pattern surrounding the text on each page. For example, open to the page where the child is kissing Baby Cakes on the nose. You might say:

> *Look at the tiny pictures above and below the words on this page. I see a bib with red, white, and blue stripes. There is also a light brown bear. I notice the small bear is the same as the bear on the opposite page. What color is the bear's sweater? Let's look at the yellow border around the edge of this page. Do you see the flowers? What colors are the petals of the flowers? Do you see the circular red center? What color are the stems and leaves?*

You may decide to follow one object, pattern, or shape throughout the book or point out different features in each illustration.

Integrate Actions

Teachers often use movement to enhance a book-sharing experience. Movement can also help active children access books. While you read Baby Cakes, help your child understand the correlation between text and actions. First, ask your little one to point to the babies and their cuddly animals in each illustration. Then, describe what they are doing. For example, on the page that says, "Yay for little Baby Cakes. Clap, clap, clap!", you might say:

> *The little boy has his Baby Cakes in his lap. They are facing each other, and they are both smiling. The little boy is clapping with his teddy bear. I can smile and clap my hands, too. This is how I clap my hands. Can you clap your hands? Let's clap our hands together!*

As you read, ask your little one to demonstrate other actions and movements shown in the illustrations.

Vary Your Reading

Reading with emphasis, or changing the inflection and tone of your voice, helps draw children into the text. Young children love songs and chants, and Baby Cakes lends itself well to a rhythmic reading. Try to keep a chanting beat or help your little one to tap the beat as you recite the words. You might even ask your child to clap, snap, or tap a foot while you read to help demonstrate the rhythm. After a few readings, you may also decide to pause at the end of the second line of each rhyme. For example, you might read:

> *"Laugh with little Baby Cakes. Ha, ha, ha! Sing to little Baby Cakes. La, la, ... [pause] la."*

As your child's speaking vocabulary grows, he will be able to fill in the missing word.

Sing Along

Teachers know that the repetition and rhythm in songs help young children internalize new vocabulary. Use the text and illustrations on the pages of Baby Cakes to spark a little song. You might sing "The Bear Went Over the Mountain", "Fuzzy Wuzzy Was a Bear", "One, Two, I Love You", or "Rock-a-bye Baby". Include any other songs or rhymes you and your little one can think of that are inspired by the illustrations or text.

Five Little Monkeys Jumping on the Bed
written and illustrated by Eileen Christelow

Text version of the classic children's counting song
Features: simple, repetitive, rhyming text; soft, colorful, active illustrations

Introduce Previewing
Teachers often preview books with children to activate their thinking before a story even begins. Start by looking at the cover of the book. Point to the title and picture. Talk about what you might be thinking as you look at the cover. You might say:

> This story is called *Five Little Monkeys Jumping on the Bed*; what do you think it will be about? Does the word Monkeys *in the title give you a hint? Who is in the picture? What ideas does that give you about what might happen in the story?*

Point out the name of the author and illustrator. You might say:

> *Eileen Christelow is the author. She wrote down the words. She is also the illustrator. She created the pictures to go along with the words.*

Recognize Letters and Words
Teachers use repetitive text and songs to introduce young children to letters and words. Small words are powerful tools for emphasizing letter recognition and introducing the concept that individual letters strung together can create familiar words. Every time the word *jumping* appears in Five Little Monkeys Jumping on

the Bed, point to it, say it, spell it, and then say it again. You might say:

> This book is called *Five Little Monkeys Jumping on the Bed*. This is the word Jumping. The letters j-u-m-p-i-n-g spell jumping. Look, here is the word jumping again. Jumping begins with the letter J. Juh, juh, J. The letter J is made with a long, curved line. We can find the word jumping on many pages of this book. Juh, juh, jumping. Can you point to the word jumping on this page? Can you help me say the letters in the word jumping?

Point to the letters as you say each one together and trace each letter with your finger. As you continue reading, pause before reading the word *jumping* to see if your child can fill in the word. To further illustrate the relationship between words and pictures, ask your child to point to a jumping monkey in the illustrations.

Predict and Pretend

Teachers often ask children to predict, pretend, ask questions, and think critically while they are reading. These are important tools for comprehension and advanced interaction between the reader and a book. As you read Five Little Monkeys Jumping on the Bed, expose your little one to language and interactive thoughts by modeling these tools. For example, on the page where the five little monkeys are asleep, you might say:

> Look, all the monkeys are finally tucked into bed. Why do you think they kept jumping on the bed? They all got hurt when they fell off the bed. Mama had to put bandages on all of their heads. Do you think they will feel better in the morning? Look at the mama now. She looks relieved that they are all finally asleep and cannot jump on the bed anymore. Do you think you would feel relieved if those monkeys were your children? I would be relieved!

It is important to note that there is no right answer to these questions. The idea is to help your child learn to think aloud and practice critical thinking. While you predict and pretend, notice how prior knowledge and past experiences influence your conversation.

Identify Colors, Patterns, and Shapes

Educators often ask young children to identify objects and patterns based on their colors and shapes. The illustrator, Eileen Christelow, incorporates many colors and patterns into the pictures in <u>Five Little Monkeys Jumping on the Bed</u>. As you share the pictures with your little one, point out and say the names of the different colors, shapes, and patterns, including pajamas, bed sheets, and chairs. For example, turn to the page when the five little monkeys first jump on the bed. You might say:

> There are a lot of colors and patterns in this picture. I notice there is an orange checkered comforter on the bed. I also notice that each of the monkeys is wearing pajamas with a different design. The first monkey is wearing pajamas with green trees. What color are the round suns? What color is the second monkey's nightgown? The third monkey is wearing pajamas with round dots. What color are the circles around the orange dots? The fourth monkey has stripes. What color are the stripes? The fifth monkey has pajamas with polka dots. What color are the dots?

You may decide to follow one object, pattern, or shape throughout the book or point out different features in each illustration.

Practice Number Sense

Books provide a platform for introducing the concept of number sense and exposing children to an early visual understanding of math. Use the pages of <u>Five Little Monkeys Jumping on the Bed</u> to play counting games. For example, on the first page, you might say:

> Look, all five of the monkeys are taking a bath. I notice that some of the monkeys have a scrub brush or a cloth and are washing their bodies. Can you count how many monkeys are washing? Yes, one, two, three monkeys are washing. The other two are playing.

> In the second picture, all five monkeys are putting on their pajamas. Some of the monkeys have their arms in the air. How many monkeys have their arms in the air? Yes, one, two, three monkeys have their arms up while they are putting on their pajamas. That means that two monkeys

*have their arms down by their sides, because three plus two
equals five.*

*In the third picture, they are brushing their teeth. Let's
count the toothbrushes in this picture: one, two, three, four,
five.* [Pause to let your child provide the next number in
the sequence if he is able.] *Are there the same number of
toothbrushes as there are monkeys?*
Together with your little one, count towels, monkeys, eyes, tears,
bandages, noses, feet, tails, pajamas, and pillows. Count anything
else you and your child can find in the illustrations.

Integrate Actions
Teachers often use movement to enhance a book-sharing
experience. Movement can also help active children access books.
While you read <u>Five Little Monkeys Jumping on the Bed</u>, help
your child understand the correlation between text and actions.
First, ask your little one to point to the monkeys, the mama, and
the doctor in the illustrations. Then, describe what they are doing.
For example, in different pictures the monkeys are jumping, lying
down, kneeling, standing, sitting, peeking over the bed, throwing
their hands in the air, and climbing. The mama and the doctor
become more frustrated as the story progresses. Ask your little one
to act out the motions (other than jumping on the bed, of course).
Following the page showing the monkey in the green nightgown
falling off the bed, you might say:
> *I am going to pretend I am on the phone; I am holding it up
> to my ear. Can you hold a pretend phone to your ear? I am
> the frustrated doctor talking to the mama. Look at my face.
> It is scrunched up and I am pulling on my hair. Those
> monkeys need to stop jumping on the bed! Can you show me
> your upset doctor face?*

You might use fun hand motions to emphasize the numbers and
actions in the story. For example, when you read the number *five*,
hold up five fingers. As you read, ask your child to demonstrate
other actions and movements shown in the illustrations.

Teachable Moment
Picture books often include an important message, or a moral, that
resonates with young children. Teachers use these stories to

reinforce specific behaviors, teach about right and wrong, or introduce a new lesson. After you read <u>Five Little Monkeys Jumping on the Bed</u>, explain to your child that beds are for resting and sleeping. You might say:

> *Even though it might seem like fun, jumping on the bed is dangerous. What can happen if you jump on the bed and fall? Yes, you could get hurt, just like the monkeys. Your body is delicate, especially your head and your neck. Why do you think the doctor becomes more and more upset during the story? Yes, the doctor wants the monkeys to be safe. So does their mama. It is important for the monkeys to listen to the mama when she tells the them not to jump on the bed.*

Vary Your Reading

Reading with emphasis, or changing the inflection and tone of your voice, helps draw children into the text. Young children love songs and chants, and <u>Five Little Monkeys Jumping on the Bed</u> lends itself well to a rhythmic reading. You can sing the classic song if you know it or make up your own if you do not. Either way, try to keep a beat, or help your little one to tap the beat as you recite the words. You might even ask your child to clap, snap, or tap a foot while you read to help demonstrate the rhythm. After a few readings, you may also decide to pause at the end of the second line of each rhyme. For example, you might read:

> *"Five little monkeys jumped on the bed! One fell off and bumped his . . .* [pause] *head."*

As your child's speaking vocabulary grows, she will be able to fill in the missing word.

Sing Along

Teachers know that the repetition and rhythm in songs help young children internalize new vocabulary. Use the text and illustrations on the pages of <u>Five Little Monkeys Jumping on the Bed</u> to spark a little song. You might sing the classic song "Five Little Monkeys Jumping on the Bed", "Ten in the Bed (Roll Over)", "Going to the Zoo", or "Pop Goes the Weasel". Include any other songs or rhymes you and your little one can think of that are inspired by the illustrations or text.

How Do Dinosaurs Say Good Night?
written by Jane Yolen, illustrated by Mark Teague

A playful look at child-like dinosaurs right before bedtime
Features: large type; one sentence on most pages;
large, detailed dinosaur illustrations

Introduce Previewing

Teachers often preview books with children to activate their
thinking before a story even begins. Start by looking at the cover of
the book. Point to the title and picture. Talk about what you might
be thinking as you look at the cover. You might say:

> This story is called _How Do Dinosaurs Say Good Night?._
> _What do you think it could be about? Does the word_
> Dinosaur _in the title give you a hint? Who is in the picture?_
> _What ideas does that give you about what might happen in_
> _the story? I noticed that the dinosaur and the mommy are_
> _both smiling. I wonder if the dinosaur is ready to say_
> _goodnight._

Point out the name of the author and illustrator. You might say:

> _Jane Yolen is the author. She made up the story and wrote_
> _down the words. Mark Teague is the illustrator. He created_
> _the pictures to go along with the words._

The inside of the cover shows different dinosaurs in their beds,
along with their names. Ask your child what she thinks these
pictures will have to do with the story.

Introduce New Vocabulary

Teachers are aware that books often include vocabulary words that are unfamiliar to children. As a result, books often expose children to words they might not hear in everyday conversations. These words can give information, make a text sound more sophisticated or more like everyday speech, or help convey emotion. The scientific name of each dinosaur in How Do Dinosaurs Say Good Night? appears somewhere on the page. Help your little one to find each dinosaur's name and pronounce it with your child. On the first page, you might say:

> *There are many kinds of dinosaurs. Look at the end of the dinosaur's bed. It says* Tyrannosaurus Rex. *That means that this dinosaur is a* Tyrannosaurus Rex. *Sometimes people call this dinosaur a T-Rex. Can you point to the words* Tyrannosaurus Rex *on the end of the bed? Let's keep reading and see what kind of dinosaur is on the next page.*

After you finish reading the book, help your little one point to each of the dinosaurs on the inside of the cover and pronounce the names. Making connections to stories is a tool that educators use to encourage critical thinking. If you come across these words in other books you share, or in another setting, remind your child that you also saw them in How Do Dinosaurs Say Good Night?.

Recognize Letters and Words

Teachers use repetitive text to introduce young children to letters and words. Small words are powerful tools for emphasizing letter recognition and introducing the concept that individual letters strung together can create familiar words. Every time the word *dinosaur* appears in How Do Dinosaurs Say Good Night?, point to it, say it, spell it, and then say it again. You might say:

> *This book is called How Do Dinosaurs Say Good Night?. This is the word* dinosaur. *The letters* d-i-n-o-s-a-u-r *spell* dinosaur. *Look, here is the word* dinosaur *again.* Dinosaur *begins with the letter D. Duh, duh, D. The lowercase letter* d *has a tall straight line and one rounded line. We can find the word* dinosaur *on many pages of this book. Duh, duh,* dinosaur. *Can you point to the word* dinosaur *on this page? Can you help me say the letters in the word* dinosaur?

Point to the letters as you say each one together and trace each letter with your finger. As you continue reading, pause before reading the word *dinosaur* to see if your child can fill in the word. To further illustrate the relationship between words and pictures, ask your child to point to the dinosaur in each illustration.

Recognize Expressions and Emotions

Illustrators often vary a character's expressions or body language in order to convey a particular emotion. In <u>How Do Dinosaurs Say Good Night?</u> the characters are very expressive. Point out the facial expressions and body language of both the dinosaurs and their parents and discuss whether the characters look sad, angry, defiant, frustrated, hopeful, peaceful, or relaxed. For example, on the page where the dinosaur falls down onto his bedcovers and cries, you might say:

> *Look at the dinosaur's mother. She wants the dinosaur to say goodnight and go to bed. I can tell by the way she is standing with her hands on her hips, her eyebrows scrunched together, and her mouth turned down that she is frustrated, or angry, with the dinosaur because he is not going to sleep. Look at the dinosaur. Is he happy or sad? Yes, he is very sad. How can you tell that he is sad? I think the dinosaur is very tired, but he does not want to go to sleep.*

As you read, mimic the expressions of the characters. You might say:

> *This is how I look when I am sad like the dinosaur* [express sadness], *but this is how I look when I am happy again* [express happiness]. *Can you show me how you look when you are sad? Can you show me how you look when you are happy?*

Make Connections

Educators ask children to make connections to stories and text in order to increase comprehension. Spend some time on each page of <u>How Do Dinosaurs Say Good Night?</u> narrating the pictures. Tell your little one what is happening and make connections. You might link the text to other books, to personal experiences, or to events in the real world. For example, each dinosaur is pictured in his room. Point out the objects in the rooms, such as a bed, books, toys, teddy bears, clothes, wall art, windows, or pets. Next point out anything in the dinosaur's room that your child also has. On the page where the dinosaur is throwing the teddy bear, you might say:

> *Look, the dinosaur has a fuzzy teddy bear. Do you have a stuffed toy? He also has a pair of blue boots next to his dresser. You have shoes, too. When do you wear your shoes? The dinosaurs name is* Pteranodon; *I can see it spelled with blocks. The dinosaur has lined up the blocks on the floor. Do you ever line up toys? Look at all the dinosaur's books. Do you have books, too?*

Making connections not only increases understanding, but also serves to honor your child's experiences, and helps your little one view stories through a personal lens.

Consider the Concept of Perspective

Teachers often use books to illustrate basic scientific concepts. The dinosaurs in How Do Dinosaurs Say Good Night? are drawn big, and yet their beds and all their toys are human size, so the objects in the rooms seem little by comparison. Point out to your little one how the large dinosaur is trying to snuggle down on a normal-sized human bed, or is holding a ball or toy that looks too small for him. Ask your child to point out other big and little items on each page. You may want to present a small toy to your child to make a comparison between his size and the size of the dinosaur. For example, on the page where the dinosaur "swings his neck from side to side", you might say:

> *Here is a ball. It is similar to the ball on the dinosaur's dresser. What do you notice about how the ball looks in your hand and how it looks next to the dinosaur? Yes, you are able to hold the ball in your hand, but it is smaller than the dinosaur's little toe! The dinosaur is much bigger than you are, so he makes all the toys look tiny.*

Identify Colors, Patterns, and Shapes

Educators often ask young children to identify objects and patterns based on their colors and shapes. The details in Mark Teague's illustrations in How Do Dinosaurs Say Good Night? offer many opportunities to point out colors, shapes, and patterns to your little one, including items of clothing, toys in the bedrooms, and sheets and bedspreads. For example, on the page with the dinosaur slamming his tail and pouting, you might say:

*Look this dinosaur's father. He is wearing a dark blue
sweater and light blue pants. What color is the sky outside
the dinosaur's window? Yes, it is also blue. This dinosaur
is dark green with brown spots. Each spot is a slightly
different shape. There is a building outside the dinosaur's
window. What shape are the yellow windows on that
building? Yes, they are rectangles. I also see a pattern on
this page. Look at the band along the top of the wallpaper:
Brontosaurus, then Tyrannosaurus Rex, then Triceratops.*

You may decide to follow one object, pattern, or shape throughout
the book or point out different features in each illustration.

Practice Number Sense

Books provide a platform for introducing the concept of number
sense and exposing children to an early visual understanding of
math. Use the pages of How Do Dinosaurs Say Good Night? to play
counting games. For example, on the page where the dinosaur
"demands a piggyback ride," you might say:

*This is an Ankylosaurus. He has scaly skin and sharp
spikes on his back and tail. He has two spikes on his head:
one, two. Let's count the spikes on his back and tail.* [Count
the spikes with your little one. Pause to let your child
provide the next number in the sequence if she is able.]
Wow! We counted twenty-nine spikes on his back and tail!

Together with your little one, count the number of sharp teeth,
long claws, big eyes, and pointy scales on the dinosaurs. You might
also count toys, pictures, books, lights, plants, pets, or anything
else you and your child can find in the illustrations.

Integrate Actions

Teachers often use movement to enhance a book-sharing
experience. Movement can also help active children access books.
While you read How Do Dinosaurs Say Good Night?, help your
child understand the correlation between text and actions. First,
ask your child to point to the dinosaur in each illustration. Then,
describe what the dinosaurs are doing to delay bedtime or to show
their parents that they are ready for bed. Ask your little one to act
out the motions. For example, when the text says, "Does a
dinosaur stomp his feet on the floor...", you might say:

I notice that the dinosaur is trying to show that he is upset. Can you show me how you would stomp if you were a dinosaur?

When the text says, "Does a dinosaur roar?", let your child roar! As you read, ask your little one to demonstrate other actions and movements shown in the illustrations.

Vary Your Reading

Reading with emphasis, or changing the inflection and tone of your voice, helps draw children into the text. The text in How Do Dinosaurs Say Good Night? is written in poetic form. Either the middle and ending words of a sentence on one page rhyme, or the end of a sentence on one page rhymes with the end of the sentence on the following page. You may choose to give extra emphasis to the rhyming words as you read. For example, you might say:

*"Does a dinosaur slam his tail and **pout**? Does he throw his teddy bear all **about**?"*

After a few readings, pause to let your child supply the rhyming words. There are also many descriptive words in the text. You may choose to change your tone and give extra emphasis as you read each of the dinosaur's actions. For example, you might read:

*"Does he **mope**, does he **moan**, does he **sulk**, does he **sigh**?"*

The first half of the book points out all the negative ways the dinosaurs might react to saying goodnight. The second half details the positive ways dinosaurs can say goodnight. You may decide to read the first half of the book with a more forceful tone and change to a more gentle tone for the second half of the book. Changing your facial expressions and body language can work with a change in voice to communicate a different perspective.

Sing Along

Teachers know that the repetition and rhythm in songs help young children internalize new vocabulary. Use the text and illustrations on the pages of How Do Dinosaurs Say Good Night? to spark a little song. You might sing "Rock-a-bye Baby" or "Lullaby and Goodnight". Include any other songs or rhymes you and your little one can think of that are inspired by the illustrations or text.

BE A LITERACY AMBASSADOR!

Children who have not been exposed to books before beginning formal schooling are at a heartbreaking disadvantage once they enter a classroom.

Now that you are trained to read like a teacher, please pay it forward and help another caregiver learn The *Bookworm Babies* Method. Here's how:

1. Post a picture on social media. Tag the photo with: #bookwormbabies, #bookwormbabiesmethod, and #literacyambassador.

2. Take a moment to write a review on www.amazon.com. Even the shortest reviews raise awareness for this mission and bring the conversational knowledge of *Bookworm Babies* to new sets of parents.

3. Pass along a copy of *Bookworm Babies* to family members, friends, colleagues with young children, or to any new parent you know. Consider purchasing one (or more) of the 20 book recommendations as a companion to *Bookworm Babies*.

4. Distribute *Bookworm Babies* to families, schools, libraries, pediatric offices, hospitals, charities, and/or organizations around the globe.

5. Visit the Literacy Ambassador page at www.bookwormbabies.com for more information.

Together we can work toward closing achievement gaps by bringing conversational book-sharing to every infant, toddler, and preschooler in our global community.

ENDNOTES

[1] Center on the Developing Child (2009). Five Numbers to Remember About Early Childhood Development (Brief). Retrieved from www.developingchild.harvard.edu.

[2] National Institute for Literacy. 2009. Early Literacy: Leading the Way to Success, a Resource for Policymakers. http://www.nifl.gov/publications/pdf/EL_policy09.pdf

[3] Literacy Promotion: An Essential Component of Primary Care Pediatric Practice, Council on Early Childhood, Pediatrics (American Academy of Pediatrics), June 2014, peds 2014-1384; DOI: 10.1542/peds.2014-1384

[4] www.pediatrics.org/cgi/doi/10.1542/peds.2014-1384

[5] U.S. Department of Education, National Center for Education Statistics 1993-275, Office of Educational Research and Improvement, National Adult Literacy Survey, April 2007 https://nces.ed.gov/pubs93/93275.pdf

[6] www.pediatrics.org/cgi/doi/10.1542/peds.2014-1384

[7] Carol A. Quick, Ed.D., Reading Books to Babies, Kids Health/The Nemours Foundation, http://kidshealth.org/en/parents/reading-babies.html?WT.ac=ctg#catlearning (May 2013)

[8] M. Caskey, M.D., B. Stephens, M.D., R. Tucker, B.A., B. Vohr, M.D., "Adult Talk in the NICU (neonatal intensive care unit) with Preterm Infants and Developmental Outcomes" (Dec 2013), Women & Infants Hospital of Rhode Island and The Warren Alpert Medical School of Brown University; Pediatrics, the official journal of the American Academy of Pediatrics; www.pediatrics.org/cgi/doi/10.1542/peds.2013-0104

[9] Widely attributed to Sir Arthur Conan Doyle

[10] www.pediatrics.org/cgi/doi/10.1542/peds.2014-1384

ACKNOWLEDGEMENTS

This ride would not have been so wild and sweet — nor so long! — had it not been for our extraordinary friendship and the fun we continue to have together.

Deepest gratitude goes to *all* our friends for their continued interest, support, questions, and encouragement. A special thanks to a patient few who traveled along an extended portion of this winding decade-long journey with us: Patrick and Tricia Brogan, Beth and Huw Bower, the ladies of the Boston Book Club, Brian and Theresa Bujdoso, the BU crew, Bob and Kate Delhome, Kamieka Gabriel, Friends of Heath, the Braun family, Heather and Mark Kerpen, Paula Machado, Brian Margis, Amy and John Mariani, Dave and Jenna Poras, Yvette "Jeffy" Ruffin, Beth Stebe, T & B, Patty and Rick Wright, and Nick Dixon and Liz Zigmont.

A special thank you for the savvy social media, permissions, legal, and editing talents of: Monique Appleton, Sara Berkson, Steffani Boudreau, Yael DeCapo, Susan Dolphin, Nancy Donahoe, Gregory Fenton, Monique Hamze, Bruce Kraysler, Andressa Oliveira, Shibani Rao, Kathryn Rogers & Amit Shah at Green Comma, and Anne Stericker.

We are deeply grateful for all our generous connectors — friends, colleagues, and networkers — who gave of their own time to help propel this mission forward: Jen Brown at Capo, South Boston, Cara Candal, Nancy Lee, Tara McCarthy of Kindrdfood, Dr. Chris Hilicki, Mneesha Nahata, Mari Passananti, Winnie Prentiss at Quarto Publishing, Susan Shaw, Kelly Sippell at the University of Michigan, Joy Olaes Surprenant at Catching Joy, Bryant and Erin VanCronkhite, and Andy Zimmer at Alibi.

Heartfelt thanks to: Mark Blumenthal, M.D., for your support of and enthusiasm for this project, and the families in your care with whom you will share it. Laurie Cestnick, Ph.D., for your contributions in the field of neuroscience and for your special attention to a few of our favorite readers. Beth Donegan Driscoll at Boston Children's Hospital for your understanding of the need for early childhood literacy support, and your recognition and support of our passion for it. Dr. Jane Lannak at the Early Childhood Learning Lab at Boston University for your notes, your advice, your love of education, and your encouragement. Vicki Milstein for your steadfast dedication to education and immediate excitement for this project. Peter Reynolds for embracing our vision, sharing your book, and supporting our journey toward a shared North Star.

Thanks also go to our global friends and fans on Facebook, Instagram, and Twitter, whose questions, comments, likes, shares, and photographs keep us motivated and help us fulfill our mission.

A special shout out to the hardworking baristas at Starbucks and at local coffee shops throughout Belmont, Boston, Brighton, Brookline, Cambridge, and Watertown, without whom this book might have taken even longer to publish.

To the wonderful book lovers at Barnes & Noble, Belmont Books, The Blue Bunny Bookstore, Brookline Booksmith, The Children's Bookshop, and Park Street Books: thank you for entertaining our questions, encouraging our explorations, and permitting our many photographs.

To you — parent, guardian, caregiver, friend, relative, teacher — thank you for reading with a child today.

Finally, words cannot properly express the appreciation we feel for our loving families.

KZA: Thank you, Bella and Ben, for all the snuggles, books, and joy you share with us, and Eric, the love of my life, for always supporting me in everything I do. Thank you, Ivan and Sally Zimmer, who from flash cards to book talks cultivated our love of reading, gave us the tools and the support to reach for our dreams, and loved us beyond reason. To Deb and Art Aulenback, the greatest in-laws and friends you can imagine, Amber, Madeline, Moira, Maren, and Mike Quirk, Thom, Deanna, Austin, Jackson, Adilyn, Michael, Christa, Quinn, Joe, Ira, Jason, Grams, and Andrew Zimmer, Kelly Hogan, Rebecca and Greg Langston, Uncle Bob D'Amore and Chris Twohig, the Kings, and the Penmans, thank you for all your feedback, questions, check-ins, moral support, and love along this journey.

DOT: All my heartfelt gratitude and respect to: Jim for your unending love and for fully embracing all our many journeys — past, present, and future. Mark and Lexi for your contagious excitement for life, and for all the stories that live through your experiences. The ever-supportive Tanya Ohanian and Jason Ohanian for decades of unconditional love, conversations, and great laughter. Phyllis Tringas, Helen Ohanian, Ronnie Ohanian, Diane Devlin, Andrea, Allan and Elizabeth Ford, Ben and Penny Fogel, Gary, Gia and Ashley Tringas, and Andy, Niki, John Andrew, Kalina and Tiana Tringas for our many years of merriment and book-related exchanges. Wendy, Peter, Jennifer and Matt Anderson, Naida Gavrelis, Kirsten, Sten, Nils and Mina Willander, and Jake Sweeney for being the best cousin group ever. The incomparable and transcendent Robert Ohanian and John Tringas. We can feel your love from here.

ABOUT THE AUTHORS

Kimberly Zimmer Aulenback and Dawn Ohanian Tringas are dedicated to supporting accessible and sustainable early childhood learning. Both hold a Master's Degree in Education and have over 25 years of teaching experience between them. As educational consultants, Aulenback and Tringas work with parents and caregivers to navigate book-sharing relationships with children, and to assist companies who wish to add educational components to their products.

Mrs. Aulenback lives just outside Boston with her husband, a daughter, who is an avid reader, and a son, who is enjoying his books and hers.

Mrs. Tringas resides outside of Boston with her husband and two book-loving children.